STUDIES

IN THE

SOCIAL ASPECTS

OF THE

DEPRESSION

Studies in the Social Aspects of the Depression

Advisory Editor: *ALEX BASKIN*

State University of New York at Stony Brook

RESEARCH MEMORANDUM ON EDUCATION IN THE DEPRESSION

By THE EDUCATIONAL POLICIES COMMISSION

ARNO PRESS

A NEW YORK TIMES COMPANY

Reprint Edition 1972 by Arno Press Inc.

Reprinted from a copy in The Newark Public Library

LC# 72-162838
ISBN 0-405-00841-4

Studies in the Social Aspects of the Depression
ISBN for complete set: 0-405-00840-6
See last pages of this volume for titles.

Manufactured in the United States of America

Preface to the New Edition

EDUCATION, perhaps the most fundamental of all American institutions, suffered sharp reductions in the harsh years of the 1930's. Determined to reduce taxes, school boards and private interest groups called for widespread cuts in school curricula. In many school districts, programs for the retarded and the physically handicapped were terminated or reduced. In some states, the salaries of teachers were cut back by legislative act, while in many localities, teachers were furloughed or dismissed. School supplies were at a minimum and school building programs ground to a halt, leaving many structures half-completed. In some urban regions, the school year was shortened while in many rural areas there was not enough money to open the schools for more than a few weeks. In Chicago, America's second city, payless paydays were more the rule than the exception, and teachers there lost their homes, their cars, their insurance policies, and, in some instances, their dignity.

The Social Science Research Council, recognizing the magnitude of the task of studying education during this period of economic contraction, called upon the distinguished scholars who constituted the Educational Policies Commission to engage in the study effort. Mindful of the fact that "history hardly warrants any assumption that there will be no similar disturbances again," the Commission worked both to examine existing conditions and to stimulate desirable changes in education. Their findings and observations are the subject of this important book.

Alex Baskin
Stony Brook, New York, 1971

BULLETIN 28

1937

RESEARCH MEMORANDUM ON EDUCATION IN THE DEPRESSION

By THE EDUCATIONAL POLICIES
COMMISSION ★ ★ ★ *Appointed by*
the National Education Association of The United States
and the American Association of School Administrators

PREPARED UNDER THE DIRECTION OF THE
COMMITTEE ON STUDIES IN SOCIAL
ASPECTS OF THE DEPRESSION

SOCIAL SCIENCE RESEARCH COUNCIL
230 PARK AVENUE   NEW YORK   NY

The Social Science Research Council was organized in 1923 and formally incorporated in 1924, composed of representatives chosen from the seven constituent societies and from time to time from related disciplines such as law, geography, psychiatry, medicine, and others. It is the purpose of the Council to plan, foster, promote, and develop research in the social field.

CONSTITUENT ORGANIZATIONS

American Anthropological Association

American Economic Association

American Historical Association

American Political Science Association

American Psychological Association

American Sociological Society

American Statistical Association

FOREWORD

*By the Committee on Studies in
Social Aspects of the Depression*

THIS monograph on research pertaining to education in the
depression is one of a series of thirteen sponsored by the
Social Science Research Council to stimulate the study of depression effects on various social institutions. The full list of titles
is on page ii.

The depression of the early 1930's was like the explosion of
a bomb dropped in the midst of society. All the major social
institutions, such as the government, family, church and school,
obviously were profoundly affected and the repercussions were
so far reaching that scarcely any type of human activity was
untouched. The facts about the impact of the depression on
social life, however, have been only partially recorded. It would
be valuable to have assembled the vast record of influence of
this economic depression on society. Such a record would constitute an especially important preparation for meeting the
shock of the next depression. Theories must be discussed and
explored now, if much of the information to test them is not
to be lost amid ephemeral sources.

The field is so broad that selection has been necessary. In
keeping with its mandate from the Social Science Research Council, the Committee sponsored no studies of an exclusively economic or political nature. The subjects chosen for inclusion were
limited in number by resources. The final selection was made
by the Committee from a much larger number of proposed subjects, on the basis of social importance and available personnel.

Although the monographs clearly reveal a uniformity of goal, they differ in the manner in which the various authors sought to attain that goal. This is a consequence of the Committee's belief that the promotion of research could best be served by not imposing rigid restrictions on the organization of materials by the contributors. It is felt that the encouraged freedom in approach and organization has resulted in the enrichment of the individual reports and of the series as a whole.

A common goal without rigidity in procedure was secured by requesting each author to examine critically the literature on the depression for the purpose of locating existing data and interpretations already reasonably well established, of discovering the more serious inadequacies in information, and of formulating research problems feasible for study. He was not expected to do this research himself. Nor was he expected to compile a full and systematically treated record of the depression as experienced in his field. Nevertheless, in indicating the new research which is needed, the writers found it necessary to report to some extent on what is known. These volumes actually contain much information on the social influences of the depression, in addition to their analyses of pressing research questions.

The undertaking was under the staff direction of Dr. Samuel A. Stouffer, who worked under the restrictions of a short time limit in order that prompt publication might be assured. He was assisted by Mr. Philip M. Hauser and Mr. A. J. Jaffe. The Committee wishes to express appreciation to the authors, who contributed their time and effort without remuneration, and to the many other individuals who generously lent aid and materials. To the Educational Policies Commission, and, particularly, to its Secretary, Dr. William G. Carr, the Committee owes special acknowledgment for the cooperative enterprise which made possible the present monograph.

William F. Ogburn, Chairman
Shelby M. Harrison
Malcolm M. Willey

The Educational Policies Commission

Appointed by the National Education Association of the United States and the American Association of School Administrators

FOREWORD

By the Educational Policies Commission

THIS is one of a series of thirteen projected monographs, all sponsored by the Social Science Research Council, each of which outlines a research program for studying the effects of the depression on some phase of society. This document deals with education; others in the series are planned to discuss consumer problems, crime, the family, health, reading habits, minority peoples, mobility of population, recreation, relief policy and practice, religion, rural life, and social work.

In accepting the Council's invitation to prepare the monograph in the field of education, the Educational Policies Commission had in mind that one of its purposes is "to appraise existing conditions in education critically and to stimulate desirable changes in the purposes, procedures, and organization of education."

Astronomers cross continents and climb high mountains in order to observe such a *natural* phenomenon as an eclipse of the sun. Is not so devastating a *social* phenomenon as a great depression at least equally useful as a theme for scientific studies which may redound to the advantage of humanity? The effects of the business cycle on schools and other educational agencies are so penetrating that the study reported here seemed a necessary step in carrying out the Commission's program of appraisal and planning.

The working bibliography collected during the preparation of this report is being published separately by the Commission.

The Commission appreciatively acknowledges the work of Dr. Jesse B. Sears, Professor of Education, Stanford University, who took a leave of absence in order to join the Commission's staff and carry forward the work on this important project.

CONTENTS

xi

Chapter I

Planning for the Study of Depression Effects

THE year 1929 brought to the business life of the country a severe shock. Symptoms of an impending economic catastrophe had been pointed out earlier by a few economists, but were declared not to exist by others. Financiers and industrialists had vaguely sensed that all was not well, but their few half-hearted warnings went largely unheeded and the crushing effects of a long depression fell upon us.

The Shock of the Depression

Whatever this calamity was at the outset, it soon became many things—a general mêlée—wherein cause and effect were confused and indistinguishable. Very early it became apparent that no individual or institution could hope to escape its influence, and that many would do well not to lose their moorings entirely. Before long, stunned from the shock and desperate from their plight, the people began to call upon the government to rescue them. The early cry was for relief from tax burdens, already heavy, and soon after for direct help to obtain food, shelter, and medical care.

Such a picture is not entirely strange to the historian nor to the economist. Our country has gone through many depressions and economists have described them. Looking back, however, one is inclined to doubt whether at the outset of the recent depression educators knew what to expect.

So great has been the recent disruption of the educational

1

service in all its parts and aspects that to statesmen and educators, alike, it has become obvious that one of the cornerstones of our entire culture, as well as of our government, has been endangered. For this reason it is not only wise but obligatory for the profession to study the effects of this depression upon education. History hardly warrants the assumption that there will be no similar disturbances again. If surface indications are correct, the forces that seem to have produced the 1929 depression are still operating.

As there has been sought through many generations a cure for certain diseases of the body, so there must be pursued search for cures for stubborn social ills. The symptoms of a serious depression, in retrospect plainly visible on every hand, should not go unobserved nor disregarded. As in bodily disease, the symptoms displayed are different at different stages. At every stage of this depression, causes are so related to effects that nothing short of the most painstaking analysis can hope to separate the two. Because the forces of education have suffered and because, so far, hope is negligible that an end has been seen to such disturbances, it is imperative to take stock.

The Terms Depression, Education, Research, and Effects

As a social and economic disturbance the term "depression" commonly refers to that portion of a business cycle in which business and industry decline below "normal" to a low point of activity, followed after a time by a period in which indexes move upward to a period of "normality." For purpose of this study the term "depression" includes the entire period in which the business indexes are below "normal."

The latest depression began in 1929 with a sudden fall of prices in the securities and commodities markets. Following this crash the decline lasted well into 1932-33, when the first signs of recovery appeared. These signs have become more convincing as figures have revealed a gradual growth in business activity, though how long it may be before normality shall have been attained is not entirely clear. The obverse of this scene is to be found in the other part of the business cycle. Business does not stop at "normal" but continues upward for a time, reaches a peak and then undergoes a decline until "normal" is reached once more. That education is more disturbed by the depression than by the prosperity end of this cycle there can be little doubt. Whether education is correct in its assumption that progress is made during the prosperous part of the cycle is a fair question. That, however, is not of concern here.

Concern is primarily with *what happened to education* during the depression. Even during prosperous times, of course, there are many forces at work that have depressing effects upon education. Forces that demand lower school taxes and salaries, fewer buildings, smaller staffs, or elimination of free textbooks are continuously at work and become doubly active during a depression. Whether school boards or legislatures formulate retrenchment policies as a result of actual economic and social pressure growing out of the depression, or as a result of the work of special pressure from vested interests, is not clear. Extra efforts by pressure groups are most likely in themselves depression phenomena.

There is interest also in reasons why education reacts as it does. Analysis of causes should go as far back as possible. The further research is pursued, the more highly refined must be definitions of terms. Here, some research deals with facts and their summation alone; other studies make comparisons and seek relationships that require careful discrimination between depression and non-depression forces and between separate elements of the depression itself. It is a part of the task of research in this field to make sure that it is depression effects that are being analyzed.

The term "education is used here broadly to include all educational forces, materials, and activities—institutional and otherwise—affecting all the people. While obviously no small monograph can lay out this wide field for research with any completeness, at least some general organization is possible. No other experiences in the past have so clearly and forcefully demonstrated that education and other social interests are closely related; that organized schools do not represent education in its entirety. Never before has it been so obvious that it matters to *all* people how well or how badly *some* of the people are being educated.

While education in other countries may be touched upon at some points, no adequate treatment of this field will be attempted. Since an elaborate study of depression effects in the field of higher education is soon to appear,[1] no attempt will be made here to cover this field in a thorough way. In this monograph the main concern, directly or indirectly, is with the schools. The relation of schools to life is a part of this, since it is from life that schools derive their purposes and meanings. Public schools are part of the philosophy of government. What the state does, therefore, is of vital concern to the schools. In turn the public school affects the state. The depression affected federal, state, and local activities that in turn affected schools in ways quite unknown in past history. All school legislation, state and national, for support, organization, functions to be served, types of schools to be available, control of staff and procedures, becomes a vital part of the field. Any legislation that deals with politics and with economics in its problems of public finance, taxation, public debt, methods of producing and distributing support, and in its creation or modification or control of schools as government services also affects education.

It is not these legal and financial contacts with the state alone, however, that constitute all the border-line contacts between edu-

[1] *Depression, Recovery, and Higher Education. A Report of Committee Y of the American Association of University Professors.* New York: McGraw-Hill Book Co. 1937

cation and life outside the school. School children and teachers are an important part of the population that constitutes the state and society. These people react to depressions as citizens, as members of various social groups, as families, and as economic units, as well as in their school capacities. The objectives they seek in school are goals characteristic of life as it is represented by the society of which they and the school are a part. They may teach and learn how to conform to, or they may criticize and learn how to alter, this world in which they live. This is sociology from one viewpoint; it is education from another.

Studies on effects of the depression on education, then, necessitate knowledge of what it does to teachers and school children and of the social conditions under which they live. Poverty, for example, may so change a child's social status that it changes his personality, making of him an entirely different sort of student than he might be under different conditions. Social, economic, and moral values have been so affected by this depression that the subject matter of much of the curriculum, especially of the social sciences, needs revision. This intimate relationship of public education to government, system of economy, and social life, applies, with but slight modification, to private and parochial education as well as to that which is tax-supported.

What has been said so far about the term "education" intends no implication that schools are docile subjects. As a mode of life as well as of government, the principles of democracy shall obtain, both for state-making and for education. By such a theory the school becomes highly responsible, not to help maintain the state, but to help maintain the principles upon which the state rests. It is not as a servant but as a part of the state that it functions. In this capacity education becomes responsible for withstanding any adverse forces stirred up by a depression. Problems proposed here have been as much concerned with what education may have done about the depression as with what the depression has done to education.

In a proper sense schools are intended to supplement life. They do this by selecting from life the material most worthy of study. Coming as it does, from a changing life, the material must be worthy of use for life in a changing society. Schools should also interpret, extend, and coordinate what may be learned only in part from life. Where the radio, public library, theater, family, and street leave off, or offer partial views, the school should take hold. Schools should evaluate what life's contacts provide. While this study is not concerned with the cinema, radio, library, club, and family as such, it is concerned indirectly with what they offer in so far as they affect for good or ill the educational work of the school.

The term "research" requires little special interpretation. It should be emphasized that while many small investigations of minor matters in education are needed to round out any such major research as this monograph proposes, it is not the purpose to stimulate casual or superficial work. A review of the wide literature on this subject leaves a realization that the great need is for facts; not unsupported opinions. There is need for analyses that go beyond surface relationships.

It is not assumed that research can establish ultimate laws for the behavior of education in a depression. Depression experience, however, should be studied in the hope that the lessons learned may be conserved for future use, even though one must be content with description, classification, and comparison, or with rough inferences and evaluations.

A comment may be offered on the term "effects" as it is used here. With such a complicated set of forces as constitute the depression, and with education almost as wide in meaning as life itself, it would seem that a study of the effects of the former upon the latter would be a doubtful task for science. However, there are many tangible data which refer to the depression and likewise to education. Whether it is needless fear or actual change in economic values that causes a school board to reduce salaries is of importance. It is true that a very considerable part of the depression's effects upon education have joined forces with other influences. Social forces and phenomena are, in the nature of things, thus interlocked. This fact must not be assumed to block, but only to complicate, the task for research.

Two main types of effects—direct and indirect—are discernible, each in wide variety. Differing more in degree perhaps than in type, they are often entangled each with the other. *Direct* effects are felt when school revenues are reduced by the depression (lowered tax roll, lowered tax rate, increased amount of tax delinquency). In turn, this low income makes retrenchments necessary, so salaries are reduced or the building budget takes the reduction and new construction ceases. In such cases cause and effect are tangible and distinguishable and their relation is obvious. *Indirect* effects are felt when, because of the depression, new educational needs are created or old needs are removed. Thus, if this depression has thrown the problem of technology into a new light, the school is forced to reinterpret its instruction program to fit the new, or the newly recognized, conditions of life. If the schools, in light of these new views, quit training boys for narrow occupational niches and provided, instead, a broad general training, it might be said that although the depression had not affected the schools directly, it had affected the need for schooling by altering the meaning of education itself.

What the depression may have done to education and to the school, directly or indirectly, brings up the question of what the school and education did about the depression. Did education fight for its place? If it fought, was it for the status quo in education, or for some adjustment and reinterpretation? Did it submit in the hope of saving its old program? The manner of reaction on the part of the school is important.

Depression lowers income; the school reacts by reducing personnel. Reduced personnel results in a cumulative story of large classes, crowded classrooms, increased chances of infection with colds, increased absences, lowered standards, lower quality of work, and finally, because of lost faith in the schools, less income from taxes. Less taxes mean less education; less education means increased danger to our basic social philosophy; and so, to our state and to our very existence. This circle of cause and effect is what concerns research.

Finally, there is the consideration of values. It cannot be assumed that effects were good or bad; that the schools reacted wisely or otherwise. The concern of research must be to state the effects it finds in terms that can be clearly understood. Where this can be done in quantitative terms, measurement is possible. Where it is in other terms, the only basis for evaluation is on the strength of an hypothesis, theory, or principle. Accordingly, research workers who are not armed with competent mastery of modern theories of education, as well as with research techniques, should not enter this realm of study.

Organization of the Field for Research

A plan for approaching the task may now be suggested. To find a research problem one must have some understanding of the entire field in which it is proposed to work; a general layout of the territory and understanding of the major enterprises operating within its different parts.

Regardless of what way is chosen, there are certain principles with reference to which the depression effects must be viewed if their significance for education is to be seen. Many of the effects can be understood only if they are followed through a long way from where they seem to strike. Depression effects that alter social forms, processes, or values outside the school may have great significance for the aims, curricula, and management of schools and yet not be seen if one looks for them in the schools alone.

With the purpose of establishing a general view of the field, and a mode of approach to its study, the following propositions are offered:

1. *Education begins with the people and will be what they desire it to be.* Concern, then, must be with any changes in the educational attitudes of the people. Their estimate of the worth of education tends to issue in laws controlling schools. Although there may be a substantial lag, eventually the people will express their desires in these matters. Whatever disturbs the course of affairs among the people tends to disturb the functioning of education. What the depression did to society outside the school, therefore, may have had the utmost significance for education.

2. *The characteristics of the group to be educated have not been constant, nor will they remain constant.* From the start in this country the group to receive training has expanded almost continuously. While reasons for this have not been fully established, this growth appears to have been related to a general social trend, delegating to education a larger and larger place in our scheme of things. If growth is thus related to general social trend, then any force that shifts that trend is likely to alter the numbers and the particular groups for which the people will provide. What has happened during and following this depression that might have such effects on society's structure, processes, or values?

3. *The purposes of education are closely related to life.* Education has to be useful or the numbers seeking it will decline. Its possible uses range from ornamental, or establishment of social status, through a long range of facilitating the work of the world, providing intellectual expression, and speculating about the unknown. In all its aspects the purpose is related to life; its values are discernible and real. How those values originate is often far from clear, but as civilization has changed, these purposes, and so the aims of the school, have changed. Here is an aspect of the recent scene for the historian to trace. The depression has brought some social changes. Are they being reflected in our educational purposes? It is by taking on such new purposes that education becomes an instrument of social progress.

4. *What is taught must be of life itself.* School subject-matter may be abstracted from life, as a theory or a formula or a symbol, but in the long run it must prove pertinent to life or be cast aside. Only the fittest things survive in the curriculum ultimately, and fittest

means fittest for illuminating life. Whatever changes the processes of life, therefore, must affect the worth of any existing curriculum. It behooves the school to keep its curriculum adjusted. To do this it is necessary to know when and where it has been thrown out of alignment.

5. *Educational machinery must keep itself attuned to the task the people want performed.* This means keeping attuned to the population to be served; to the appropriate educational purposes of different groups; and to the demands of the various curricula. Organization and administration do not exist for themselves but only to facilitate education. They are none the less real for this. There must be laws establishing authority. There must be organization. There must be support and business operations and housing. All this should change as the needs for education change. If change in the social trend changes its task, then the school machine should reflect those changes. It is an important function of educational leadership to reveal these changes to the people. Has this depression brought changes of a caliber that warrant changes in the school machinery?

These are five points of view from which the effects of this depression may be examined. The first is, in a sense, the background for the other four. It will bear special study.

Educational purposes throughout the country, the school population, curricula, and organization all are widely varied. There are many types of educational enterprise. While they all belong to all the people, they are created and controlled in many ways, and to some extent each has an independent origin and history. Despite the many connections, through law, traditions, and general understanding, which each may have had with the other units in the greater scheme of education, these different types may have responded differently to depression forces.

As a partial analysis of this complex it may be noted first, that educational work is carried on under three major divisions:

1. Public schools—state controlled

2. Parochial schools—church controlled

3. Private schools—privately controlled

Because these classes are rather clearly distinguishable, such a classification offers a useful basis for delimiting studies of how they were affected by the depression. This does not mean that studies could not often profitably work horizontally through the three classes. What happens to income, debt, operating and maintenance costs, and curricula, are illustrations of points where depression effects would likely be similar in many respects. The worth of careful comparative studies of the three types of schools during and following depressions is obvious. The point noted here is that there are good reasons why each of the groups may have been affected similarly, yet reacted differently in depressions. Such fundamental differences cannot properly be overlooked by research in the field.

Further, each of these groups operates in several fields of instruction. In each of these there are elementary, secondary, higher, and special education subdivisions that make more differentiation possible. Each of these fields is, to a degree, specialized, regardless of any common system of support or control. Depression influences would strike them differently. What happens, for example, to the elementary curriculum during depressions may be very different from what happens to that of the secondary or higher field. Accordingly, depending upon the choice of the aspect or phase of education it is desired to trace, this classification suggests a further means for delimiting study. A slightly different division of the field for any one unit in the above groups may be useful:

1. What the depression did to education or to one of its institutions (say the public junior college or the endowed college)

2. What education (the people, the institution) did about it

The depression effects may be viewed in either of these two sets of terms. The story of reduced salaries may be of interest either as injury wrought to the schools or part of the method whereby the people reduced the burden of cost as one means of saving the schools. These two points of emphasis may be carried together in the study of many problems, though often one or the other will be of special interest. The depression stimulated education at innumerable points and in innumerable ways. One may ask what the depression did to any purpose, process, phase, aspect, or unit of education. Similarly, when one asks what the people did about it, one may have in mind the federal, state, and local governments; the church and other social or economic organizations; private enterprise, philanthropy, research agencies. To trace the history of any one of the federal relief activities, or to study any one line of retrenchments made by city school boards, would provide a suitable unit for study.

One other step in analysis may prove helpful. Even though the history of depression effects upon every separately managed institution ought to be written for the benefit of that institution, more often it will be upon a single part of an institution or system of schools that interest will center if the study is to be widely useful. This suggests an analysis of education from the standpoint of those who must shape its purposes and policies and direct its activities. The major tasks of making and operating the scheme of education might be described as follows:

1. To keep the philosophy of education (social, political, economic, intellectual) in process of rebuilding for public, private, and parochial schools—each separated into elementary, secondary, higher, and special schools.

2. To express this philosophy in legislation and regulations necessary to give form and direction to activities in these various divisions of education.

3. To formulate programs of instruction that reflect this philosophy and the intent of these laws for each type of educational activity.

4. To establish and maintain a staff of trained technical workers to carry this program into effect in each of the educational units.

5. To establish and maintain properties suited to the housing and equipment of the various groups to be educated.

6. To bring these philosophies, laws, instructional programs, technical workers and properties into form for action, and to direct their operation.

A further breaking down of the field might be desirable. For instance, there might be a desire to know what effect depressions have had on the teaching force. Many lines of inquiry might be tested separately with such hypotheses as that depressions tend:

1. To cause a more rapid and a greater turnover, followed by an unusually large net decline, in the number engaged in teaching.

2. To cause a decline in quality of staff. Younger teachers will more often be the ones dismissed. Summer training for those in service will decline because of expense. The staff will become older and so contain relatively more of the group who have passed their highest efficiency.

3. To result in higher requirements for certification. Supply will greatly exceed demand, and people will train more extensively for the field.

4. To lower the standard of living for teachers. Cost of living may not go down as fast as salaries, and financial obligations of teachers tend to be greater through having to contribute to more public calls for charity and by having more dependents.

Any one of the major functions outlined above offers a like possibility for the formulation of hypotheses. For instance, regarding school properties the following hypotheses might be proposed:

1. Depressions entail property shortages equivalent to total depreciation during the period, plus all additions required for growth of school population during the period.

2. School debt limitations in law tend to break down during depressions; or the reverse, that depressions cause people to enforce additional statutory controls over public debts.

3. The credit of school districts stands depressions better than does that of municipalities.

4. School property obsolescence accumulates during depressions at exceptionally rapid rates (due to extreme and rapid changes in educational programs) and remains as a relatively permanent setback to housing service.

For the field of administration, such hypotheses as the following might be proposed:

1. Inefficient systems of school support tend to be replaced during depressions. The general property tax, when used as the major basis of support; local support which bears a high percentage of cost; annual or biennial appropriations by local, county, or state lawmaking bodies, would be illustrations.

2. New laws tend to place new limits upon the powers of taxing bodies.

3. Depressions tend to result in elimination of recently developed units, features, or aspects of the school service and to leave behind the old. This is apt to mean that progress is retarded.

A skeleton summary of these several analyses of the field may serve as emphasis that this large field cannot be approached as a single problem. The field is made up of too many independent units, each of which is largely independent or easily separated from the others, and each of which must have responded somewhat independently to the depression.

Stated in outline, the following viewpoints, principles of procedure, and divisions of the field appear:

1. For effects of the depression upon education—
   a. Education may be viewed as a social process
   b. Education may be viewed as an institution
   c. Effects of the depression may be direct
   d. Effects of the depression may be indirect

2. To direct search and aid discrimination, general guiding principles are as follows—
   a. Education begins with the people
   b. School population is not fixed but changes with social trends
   c. The purposes of education are found in the nature and processes of the civilization of the time
   d. What is taught must be of value in the culture of the time
   e. Educational machinery must be designed and operated in light of educational purposes, materials, and personnel

3. As to creation, support and control, educational enterprises may be classified as—
   a. Public, governmental, institutional

   b. Parochial, church, institutional
   c. Private institutions
     (1) Philanthropic institutions
     (2) Profit-producing institutions

4. As to fields of operation, there are—
   a. Elementary—for children
   b. Secondary—for children and youth
   c. Higher—for youth and adults
   d. Special—for various age groups and groups with widely varied needs and interests. Adult education is an important aspect of this area.

5. The units of activity in educational enterprises are at times—
   a. Single institutions—as a private high school, an endowed college, an endowed research institution
   b. Systems of schools—as district, county, state; or, church or private system

6. In a study of any one unit, whether a single institution or a system, the work centers about certain major problems such as—
   a. Determining objectives
   b. Establishing laws, regulations, and policies
   c. Organizing and directing
   d. Developing a program of service
   e. Developing and maintaining a staff
   f. Housing and equipping the enterprise

7. Depression effects may be viewed in terms of—
   a. What happened to education in any of its parts or aspects
   b. What the people (directly or through some branch of the government, or school authorities) did about it

8. Depression effects upon education may be studied by selecting problems—
   a. Within one unit of the above outlines under 3, 4, and 5
   b. Within common features or aspects of the units
   c. A vertical section through most or all of the units

From these analyses it is clear that a research problem in this field may have to do with a phase, an aspect, a feature, or a unit of educational service; or with the social facts and phenomena that give rise to the service. In the presentation of the problems it is not presumed that every problem has been listed. At most, only samples are offered. To bring these into some order, the above skeleton picture of the field has been kept in mind and consistent with that analysis a classification of the problems is used that takes note of essential functional areas of the field.

The Field for Study

In bodily disease, a cause may often operate for a long time before it is discernible to any but expert observers, and even to them only by exhaustive search. So, it seems to have been with this depression. It is difficult, therefore, to tell where in point of time to begin study.

Educators might leave to politics, economics, and sociology the task of finding and removing the causes of depressions. Yet, where does education begin? Clearly, it begins in the theory of the state, in the social philosophy upon which our entire society and its culture rest, and it operates within the economic system that governs all business, public and private, of that society. Whether education is publicly supported, privately endowed, or earns its way, whether it is formalized in institutions or is incidental to the mere processes of living, it lies within the realm and must be shaped largely within the limits of the controlling philosophies—political, economic, social—of the people it serves.

Education is not merely submissive, nor should it dominate, but inevitably it must bear responsibility for helping to illuminate the phenomena out of which these philosophies are made, evaluated, and remade. This responsibility of education is reflected clearly in the program it offers and in the processes by which it operates. Its claims upon the public purse, its curricula, its organization, all reflect the theories basic to the society it serves. Education cannot ignore the economics of taxation and public spending; it cannot ignore the political question of what services—what educational services—our government shall render; it cannot ignore the manner of life among the people—

their customs, conventions, proprieties, traditions. All these are the background and starting point for what education should do.

This brief interpretation of the nature of the depression and of the province of education serves merely to suggest the intimate relationship between education and each of the major social sciences; and so, to indicate the close relationship of this monograph with the other monographs in the series. As a part of the social mechanism of democracy, education, both in its purposes and in its form, must be sensitive to any serious disturbances of the social life. This depression has created such a disturbance. Education has been affected seriously in all its parts and aspects. It is the province of this study, then, to inquire concerning the effects of the depression not on the schools alone, but over the entire field of education. The depression is part of a social trend and not something totally independent of the past and future. The schools and education are within this trend and not static and unchanging.

The Plan of Treatment

The effects of the depression most of concern are reflected both in the changes produced in education and in what the people or the schools did about it. Through proposed researches, the purpose here will be to try to bring to light any serious problems that have been left to education by this disturbance. Some of these are studies that take stock of changes, good or bad; others of evaluating what was done, or the consequences of neglect; and last, but certainly not least, of how to attack problems yet unsolved.

In such a large field for a review of this kind, many possibilities were open. The one chosen applies the logic most in use in the study of education, in writings within the field, and in the practical organization of educational service. The general topics for the eight chapters embodying the problems proposed for research are:

Historical and comparative problems
Theory and philosophy of education
Student personnel
The curriculum or program of instruction
Staff personnel
Organization and administration
Finance and business management
Scientific and professional activities

The problems presented were systematically gathered over a period of some weeks, during which time literature in this field was reviewed, conferences were held with authors of other monographs of this series in order to delimit the field, and correspondence was held with a few recognized experts interested in this problem.

From the standpoint of research, the literature comprised in the bibliography of some 1,600 titles, soon to be published by the Educational Policies Commission, was a bit disappointing. It does embody evidence of substantial activity within the profession concerning depression effects on the schools. It reflects what was done to the schools and to education in a broader sense. It not only reveals what the people and the schools were doing about their difficulties, but also much speculation as to cause and cure. Of careful research, however, it shows a very small amount. Consequently many problems have been presented in this monograph primarily as questions and have not been developed in the more extended form. Enough of them are stated as formal hypotheses so the readers will not be misled by the brief and informal setting in which some of the others appear.

In presenting the problems two groups of readers have been kept in mind, viz., advanced students and professional research workers, in the social sciences generally and in education in particular. Because education is an applied social science, there is little conflict of interest and certainly very much in common between these two groups of research workers, though at present each of them is too little acquainted with what the other is doing.

No attempt has been made to make this a treatise on education, and certainly none to make it a treatise on the social sciences. Also, it is not a systematic review of the effects of the depression on education. It proposes plans for researches that are required as a foundation for a treatise on this latter subject. In preparing these plans, and to avoid making a dull catalog of questions, effort has been made to give the questions some educational setting. All questions are not of equal importance; some, quite easy to ask, are impossible to answer satisfactorily. Views on education are offered here only as a basis for making clear some problem or group of problems.

Nor is this a treatise on research method. It does, however, provide some assistance in making an approach to the problems. To this end, effort has been made, not only to give the issues adequate interpretation from the educational and social viewpoint, but to present sample hypotheses set up for research attack, with some directions as to methods and sources. It has not been the purpose to do all the things required but only enough to suggest a mode of attack. These problems offer a wide sampling of the field, of the sources to be drawn upon, and of research techniques. In all cases, however, they were selected because they were regarded as important problems.

Chapter II

Historical and Comparative Problems

IN THE study of depression effects upon education the need for perspective is obvious. What happens in one country may not happen in another; or if it does, may happen in quite a different way. Yet, when a common form of disaster strikes all countries alike, it is apparent that the experience of one may have value for another.

The Place of Historical and Comparative Study

Continuity in social affairs may be explained by the overlapping in time of the lives of individuals, by the force of traditions, customs, and institutions, and by continuous and identical conditions and circumstances. The past is not always suited to the present or future, and never is all of it worth saving. The present acts as judge in a continuous sorting process by which some things are saved and some discarded. Thus, if the present is greatly disturbed, as by a depression, existing and past values, with their forms and channels of expression, will be thrown into new perspective and more choice will be needed as to what is to be preserved. If a new problem arises during the period of disturbance, the present has only its own imagination, its accumulation of wisdom and understanding, and its instruments from the past with which to solve it. These instruments often are the more actively applied with the result that future direction shifts only slightly from the trend of the past.

It is not assumed that all parts of the schools' recent depression experiences are equally difficult or important for study. At many points the impact has been direct and has issued in tangible form; at others, it has been intangible in its effects. Similarly, as features of the total situation, the importance of these experiences ranges from temporary and casual to relatively permanent and fundamental. If these various effects can be brought into some perspective—temporal, institutional, social, economic, political, and educational—it should indicate the direction of travel and remove from memory at least some of its misfortunes. Further, if by study of its many aspects, ways can be found to project future trends through such disturbances, the schools would be saved many shocks otherwise certain.

As an approach to the historical study of this and of earlier like periods, it is wise to distinguish between the school and education as viewed more broadly, between the social machine or institution and the processes and products of learning. The institution might be greatly altered without seriously altering results to the learner. Vice versa, much might happen to alter the child's educational needs, interests, attitudes and reactions; thus much might happen to his education, without disturbing seriously the institution. The effects of a depression must not be assumed to exist inevitably for the one because they have been proven to exist for the other.

If the goal is to provide perspective in meeting future depressions, how best may the history of this period be approached and developed? Letting the facts speak for themselves by describing and recounting in detail all that has happened; checking for time, place, and circumstance; and where possible measuring for intensity or amount, would be one way. To guess at effects, causes and implications; to set up hypotheses and examine facts to test them, would be other ways. Some amount of the former usually is necessary before good guessing can begin. An hypothesis is not a wholly random guess or explanation but one that rests upon some basic understanding.

First of all, historical studies of this period should regard the depression as an economic incident. Using reliable economic indexes, they should note when the depression began, when the low point was reached, and when recovery was achieved. The research of the economist provides a temporal and economic framework, against which the effects upon education can be located and examined.

In making comparative studies, care should be exercised that fact be not confused with interpretation. Salaries may have fallen farther from the pre-depression norm in one country than in another. That would be fact. To interpret its effect upon the teachers' standard of living, upon their morale, or upon their ability to continue summer-school study or to travel, would be quite a different thing. Yet, some inferences can be drawn from comparative data.

Types of Historical Problems

Any particular feature of depression behavior could be studied historically. The question here is what kinds of studies are needed, or what one might hope to gain by such studies. We know in general that depressions have many common characteristics in their effect on enterprises dependent upon public revenue; also, they are likely, if long continued, to affect the enterprise regardless of what the source of support may be, public or private, philanthropy or current earnings. Pitkin's study[1] of the effects of earlier depressions on education leads to the conclusion that in America school revenues were not lowered except in very severe depressions. In fact, in depression times people spent relatively more than in normal times for public education. Whether this was due to any peculiarity of earlier depressions or depression psychology, or to the general growth of economic

---

[1] Pitkin, Royce Stanley. *Public School Support in the United States During Periods of Economic Depression*. Brattleboro, Vermont: Stephen Daye Press. 1933. Pp. 143

strength is a different question. Pitkin concludes that it has been the latter. He calls attention, also, to the growth of schools and to increase in numbers of pupils. His figures indicate, however, that in previous depression periods the people actually have assumed heavier tax burdens for schools; that reductions in school revenues were relatively less than were those for other government services; and that in many cases teachers' salaries were increased during depressions in the nineteenth century. This study is more than adequate to show the possibilities of such historical and financial research. There is room for other studies, either of special sources of school income or of special classes of expenditures, covering the country either by regions or as a whole. Such studies would contribute to the social, financial, and political, as well as to the educational, history of the country.

A second field of interest for historical treatment would deal with the growth of the school population.[2] There is room for intensive study, not only of the numerical magnitude, but also of the social and educational composition of the school population. Who, as well as how many, went to school; to what type and grade of school; what age groups; what sex divisions; from what occupational groups? Did frontier and older communities respond alike? Did trends vary by states? Did rural and city populations behave alike?

A third field for historical studies would be that of school legislation. In these periods what was the nature of state and national legislation affecting schools? Statutes would be a useful source. Was there little or much legislation? Upon what and how did legislation reflect depression pressures?

A fourth field would be that of the instructional program. What happened to textbooks; to curricula? What new depar-

[2] See: Edwards, Marcia. *Relation of College Enrollment to Economic Depression in the United States, 1890 to 1930.* University of Minnesota. 1931. This report shows fluctuation from normal trends of enrollment in 96 colleges.

tures—subjects, courses, curricula, types of schools or educational activities—occurred during the depressions?

A fifth field would be that of organization and administration. State and local school systems have grown to great com-
plexity. Has their growth or any feature of it been halted or
stimulated during depression times? Were new types of educational services begun or were old ones dropped? Personnel,
properties, public relations—all suggest problem areas.

A sixth field might be that of scientific and professional activities. Has the output of scientific and philosophical writing
varied from the usual in such periods? Have new problems or
new forms of treatment arisen during or following depressions?
Of the profession, what of its membership and the activities of
its organizations?

Sample Historical Problems

The following problems are illustrations of the six types of
research suggested previously. The purpose here is to suggest
definite pieces of research and to indicate the procedure necessary to define the project and put the study under way. When
a problem is being set up for study it almost always happens that
other studies suggest themselves. It will be seen that this is
true of the problems here presented.

PROBLEM 1

*Do depressions tend to give rise to new movements and to
new developments in education?*

During this depression certain educational developments that
may have been exceptional have been seen, among which are:

1. A great expansion in adult-education activities

2. The initiation of nursery education on a large plan

3. The creation and spread of a special type of education as a feature

of the National Youth Administration or the Civilian Conservation Corps program

4. Stimulus to experimental colleges, junior colleges, and high schools

Intensive study of any one of these projects would provide a profitable line of inquiry. Here, however, the question concerns the influences that gave rise to these and other important developments in education. Why did not the needs back of these appear sooner? It may be a coincidence that they attracted attention in this depression; yet, somewhat similar relationships followed the depression of 1893, when the high school entered a period of remarkable expansion, and still earlier, in 1837, when Horace Mann did his great work for free schools.

Since history shows numerous instances in which important developments began in, or followed closely, depression periods or other crises, one is tempted by the hypothesis that: When the American people have suffered severely in some catastrophe they show a tendency to use education in unusual new ways as one means of settling their difficulties. Investigation should test that hypothesis.

The importance of such a study is obvious. If the hypothesis is true, then there is special reason why every available unit of research power should be put to work during a depression to find the needs behind such innovations. Still more, if the hypothesis is true, it suggests that a host of important educational needs go unnoticed until distress brings them forcibly into view. Research, therefore, should start earlier, for such movements as the growth of schools in the "thirties" or the spread of high schools in the "nineties." Research should rest upon something more permanent and fundamental than mere temporary distress. The need for such development undoubtedly was there before any depression period. Finally, if this hypothesis is true, it shows clearly that education is lagging far behind where it should be; that most of the time it is ignoring important needs.

Furthermore, once the relationship is established, there is the converse of this hypothesis—that during prosperous times a substantial lag accumulates between real educational needs and the school program. This raises still a further question: Does a depression enable education to recognize and thus discard useless aims and practices?

Assuming that the hypothesis is worthy of study and remembering that it is seeking *tendencies to relationship* and not *perfect agreement* between depressions and new educational developments, approach to the study would call for these steps:

1. Review studies that contribute both general background and specific facts to the problem.[3]

2. Establish the dates of major business cycles with their phases.[4]

3. Establish the origin and period of growth for each of the more important ideas and movements in the history of American education.[5]

4. Wherever a temporal relationship seems to exist, study the possible relationship of depression effects to the factors that seem to have given rise to the educational movements.

Pitkin's study offers substantial evidence on a number of points, but for the most part the facts called for should be mined out from other sources:

1. The origins of educational movements would be discussed in the literature current at the time. The daily press, and lay and profes-

---

[3] Pitkin, Royce Stanley. *Public School Support in the United States During Period of Economic Depression.* Brattleboro, Vermont: Stephen Daye Press. 1933. Pp. 143

[4] Clark, John Maurice. *Strategic Factors in Business Cycles.* New York: H. Wolff. 1934. Pp. 238

[5] Cubberley, E. P. *Public Education in the United States.* Revised edition. Boston: Houghton Mifflin Co. 1934. Pp. 782

sional journals would be the place to obtain some idea of what the people thought they wanted and what they tried to do.

2. Statutes and the various supporting literature, such as House and Senate journals, the *Congressional Record,* and corresponding state papers would reveal final legal adoption of any important movement as a part of the scheme of education.

3. Official reports of city, state, and national school officials would reveal the nature of any such movement through statistical or factual discussions.

4. Proceedings, yearbooks, and journals of professional and scientific societies devoted to the study of education.

In studying this problem one would readily think of such important educational developments as the start of academies, high schools, state universities, normal schools, experimental stations, technical and industrial education, women's colleges, kindergartens, junior high schools and junior colleges; and of important periods in their expansion. The growth in school population by divisions and by types of schools could be plotted by years and checked against depression periods. Similar treatment could be applied to data on expenditures, school property values, and number of teachers employed, using all as evidence of trends in growth or as evidence of the response of the people to the new school developments. The location of such movements as the spelling bee, the lyceum, the singing school, the Chautauqua, the Sunday school, adult education, child labor laws, compulsory attendance laws, reform schools, public and traveling libraries, school consolidation, medical inspection, mental testing, and the school survey suggest the reach of such studies.

Such movements as the teaching of the effect of alcohol and narcotics; enforced teaching of the constitution; flag salute by school children; and teachers' oaths of allegiance have become very influential. Are any such movements related to past depressions in any way?

PROBLEM 2

What types of educational legislation accompany and follow business depressions?

This question is pertinent if the theory of how education is related to social life is sound. If a depression seriously affects important balances in the social order, it thereby creates social problems, and these, in turn, may affect the objectives and the program of the school. These social problems may even call for entirely new educational developments, or make useless some of the prevailing practices. When one's social status has been changed, as by becoming poor or rich, obscure or prominent, one's educational outlook (one's feeling of need for education) is changed. When many people are thus changed at one time some actual legal adjustment is likely to follow. Legislation lags, perhaps, but tries to stay close to social need, or at least close to society's feeling of need.

The recent depression has made clear how quickly social unbalance can be effected. It has shown how active education becomes as a social force. In such periods education seems more ready to criticize itself, and finally, even to set aside any part of itself that becomes ineffective and to enter upon various new projects not thought of before. If such change is a reasonable expectancy, it is further predictable that the change will take note of the social disturbance in some way. That is, it will tend to bring the scheme of education into better adjustment with social need for education.

A business depression brings unemployment. If this is on a large scale and lasts long, it will destroy credit, reduce or destroy business, industry, and commerce, and lead to government relief activities. At such times the worth of one's education, economic and social, is tested anew and is likely to be deflated and set down under a new value. The question with which any educational legislation must start out is based upon this new value. Among other things, the present CCC camps strongly suggest that the prevailing scheme of secondary education had little attraction for all too large a group of young men, who, under depression circumstances and with social values quite disarranged, were presented with educational opportunity in a new form.

If the historian can reveal what cross currents of social forces ran in each of the major depressions, and what major social changes resulted, then an analysis of the school legislation during or closely following those periods would provide opportunity to test the following hypothesis: When depressions cause major social disturbances there will follow types of legislation that represent attempts to adjust the state's educational program to new educational needs.

Such a study would be concerned equally with legislation repea'ed, amended, or enacted. The steps in such a study would be:

1. Establish dates for the depressions to be studied, as noted above

2. List the major social problems resulting from each, as set forth by historians and economists

3. Select for study states representative of various social and economic types

4. List and classify all acts repealed or amended and all new statutes[6]

5. Check, depression by depression, the types of acts in each case against the social problems

On the economic side, the hypothesis might be: Depressions tend to stimulate public spending for new or newly adjusted educational projects. Pitkin's study bears upon this but does not attempt to prove it.

This same plan of study might be applied to a review of the

[6] The U. S. Office of Education and the National Education Association have published from time to time digests of state legislation affecting education.

regulations of state boards of education through which the state administers its school laws. Such boards are far from equal in the powers they exercise, but many of them are powerful administrative bodies and their decisions affect a wide territory. Certification of teachers, graduation, textbooks, libraries, laboratories, the curriculum and its administration, and many aspects of school management are under the board's direction. Obviously their regulations would reflect changes made to bring the schools into alignment with society's new needs.

PROBLEM 3

How has the educational profession reacted to depressions?[7]

From early times there have been national, state, and local organizations of teachers in this country. Some of them have a continuous history covering half to three-quarters of a century. Professional publications, some of them scientific and others news magazines and house organs for associations of educators, have recorded the problems, attitudes, and activities of those concerned with education. In these magazines, volumes of proceedings, bulletins and yearbooks, there should be records to show how organized groups of educators pointed the way for educational adjustments during and following depressions. Have they provided leadership individually through their published articles? Have they organized effort to direct activities and even legislation to meet the pressing needs of the schools in such times?

During the present period the National Education Association formed a committee to carry on a service devoted to the task of interpreting the educational situation to the people. In many in-

---

[7] While belonging also in Chapter VIII this problem is an exceptionally good one for historical treatment. A more intensive study for the current depression may be quite useful as well.

stances local and state groups were formed for similar purposes. Even a casual view of the published output of these groups reveals that they were motivated by no narrow or selfish purposes, but by a desire to prevent serious loss to the cause of education. The force of this leadership in the recent depression was powerful and obvious. Is this the way the profession generally acts? Can the public rely upon teachers' organizations to fight intelligently and forcefully for the cause of education whenever that cause is endangered?

It is worthwhile to try to determine, by a study of depression periods, how educators have reacted as a group. A choice from three hypotheses or a combination of them could be made: (1) that teachers become active for self alone, to hold their jobs and salaries; (2) that they tend to be relatively inactive and wait for leaders from outside the profession to point the way; or (3) that they make intelligent and united effort to safeguard the educational interests of children and of society. Research would not attempt to defend any one thesis, but would check all of them against the facts.

To those directing educational organizations such a study would be useful as a basis for planning. To the profession as a whole, it would be of advantage to know what would be revealed by such a study.

The sources suggested above are readily available in libraries: publications of the National Education Association and its departments; bulletins (issued monthly) of the American Association of University Professors, and of the American Federation of Teachers; the *Yearbooks* of the National Society for the Study of Education, and of the National Society of College Teachers of Education; proceedings of state teachers' associations; official reports of national, state, and local educational executives; reports of presidents of universities, colleges and teachers' colleges; and the professional magazines and books. Some of these publications are statistical and interpretative reports; some are media for scientific studies; others emphasize opinion, and still others, news. Their respective value for this study would vary.

Other Historical Problems

If problem 3 referred to government agencies other than educational, instead of to the profession, the question would be one of equal interest. In this and in previous depressions, education has been a very great concern of government.

What have statesmen said about education during times of depression? Presidents have spoken often on this subject, and so have many other political leaders. What has been the nature of their advice to the people? It would be possible to select the depression periods for study, then to select the statesmen whose pronouncements were believed to be worthy of study and finally to collect and analyze their comments upon education.[8]

What have the important editorial writers said? Here is an influential group of thinkers and writers whose views would be of great importance. The results of their work could not be measured easily, but they could be assembled, analyzed, and characterized. Their view of the nature and place of education during any of the depressions would be worth knowing.

What happens to educational movements that develop during these depression times? The junior high school movement has been through several depressions. Teacher training; curriculum revision; extension education; compulsory attendance; part time or continuation schools; child study; school survey; and mental and physical testing are other samples.

What happens to newly added school subjects? In the latest depression a severe cut was made in the list of recently developed subjects. Was this true in other depressions? Art, home

---

[8] Consult, for example, the index (bound separately for each Congressional Session) under "Education" of the *Congressional Record*. References here would be to speeches, hearings, and legislation that concerned federal interest in education.

economics, household arts, manual training, music, physical education, nature study, and elementary science are suggested as sample subjects.[9] Finally, a study of effects of past depressions upon salary trends might supplement what Pitkin's study on this subject revealed.

Some Comparative Problems

PROBLEM 1

A comparative study of the educational features and worth of CCC camps and those of the German work camp (Arbeitslager).

The two organizations are not identical in origin nor in detail of support and control, but in important ways they are the answers given by the American and German peoples and governments, respectively, to the question of what to do with a vast number of unemployed young men who, because of social and economic conditions, were without means of support. In a sense, each of these projects is an expression of the general theory of government in vogue. Education was not the primary concern at the outset.

By a program of responsible service in an active institution, both of these projects offer experience that has educational value. In addition they offer an opportunity for study and instruction. The formal education work is substantially different from that of schools for corresponding groups. These new agencies have grown rapidly. Their worth to the young men who participated in them should be studied.

The points of comparison would need to be fixed clearly. Certainly the place of educational service as a function of the

---

[9] See, for example: Curtis, Francis D. "Some Effects of the Depression upon the Teaching of Science." *School Science and Mathematics* 34: 345-60, April 1934. See also: Williams, Jesse F. "Physical Education and the Depression." *Research Quarterly of the American Physical Education Association* 4: 9-14 March 1933

institution would be the first point. The placement and flow of authority covering the school unit—that is, the limitations under which the service could operate—would be of primary importance before further comparisons could be made. A second point of comparison might cover the educational worth of the routine, the contacts of social life, and the work. The educational value could not be exactly measured, but that for one could be set alongside of that for the other in descriptive terms and a judgment could be formed. A third point could be the educational activities themselves. Are they voluntary or compulsory? How many participate in them? Organization for study; aims and objectives; curricula or activities; methods of work; books and equipment; check up and records—on all these features some plan of comparison could be worked out.[10]

PROBLEM 2

How did the depression affect teachers' salaries in America as compared with other countries?[11]

Any group of countries could be selected for study. As a first step it would be desirable to establish the dates marking various stages in the business cycle in the countries compared. With these should be compared the dates marking the beginning of retrenchment, low point, and the beginning of recovery in education. Against these two sets of facts could be set the dates mark-

---

[10] For information on the CCC see reports of the Director of Emergency Conservation Work. See also: Oxley, Howard W. *Education in Civilian Conservation Corps Camps.* Washington, D.C.: Civilian Conservation Corps, May 1936. Pp. 11. Mimeo. For data on the German work camps (*Arbeitslager*) see: Taylor, John Wilkinson. *Youth Welfare in Germany: A Study of Governmental Action Relative to Care of the Normal German Youth.* Baird-Ward Co., Nashville, Tenn.: 1936. Pp. 259. Also see: Wilhelm, Theodor and Grafe, Gerhard. *German Education Today.* Institute of International Education, 2 W. 45th Street, New York, N.Y. 1936. Pp. 21-27

[11] What is said here may serve for such a study for this country or for a given state as would be called for in Chapter VI on teacher personnel.

ing corresponding points in the salary changes which occurred.

The next part of the study would be to determine the extent of salary reductions in the selected countries. This would be a substantial study for any one country. Several figures would be needed as a basis for interpreting reductions. A lower salary budget would be possible either by reduction of wages, by dismissal, or by changing workers. It would be desirable, therefore, to consider salary retrenchment both as a reduction in a budget item, and as an actual cut in individual salaries.

In such a study two major facts would be established:

1. That reduction of salary budget had or had not been effected. If so, whether it had been brought about—
   a. by reducing the number employed
   b. by maintaining the number, but employing relatively more in the lower, and relatively fewer in the upper, salary brackets.

2. That actual salaries had or had not been reduced. Salaries held constant could be treated as a reduction or not, as desired. In effect it would be a reduction only where contracts are based upon a schedule providing increases. It might be counted as a "reduction" or as an "omission of increase due." Where one is concerned with a large country it will be found that practice varies widely from place to place, except in countries where one salary schedule operates for the entire country or where action is always in terms of the schedule rather than persons or employees. In the United States there are so many independent controls over salaries in different states, counties, townships or districts, and methods of school support vary so widely that it is evident salary reductions would be effected very early in some places and very late in others. In comparing countries such facts should not be overlooked.

In the United States there are districts with, and other districts without, salary schedules. Then, too, there are districts having salary schedules covering some, but not all, groups of school employees. Comparison between countries should be made in terms of what is most typical. This basis might be the median salary reduction for a given group, say secondary teachers, in districts of a given class. If reductions in salaries of elementary school principals in cities of a given population group in the United States were compared with like reductions in similar population centers in England, France, or Germany, for example, the comparison would be a fair one.[12]

The amount of salary reduction or of budget retrenchment could be handled by the index method, using the salary of some one year as a base. Let the 1929 median salary be the base for the group studied (as elementary teachers in cities having a population from 30,000 to 50,000) and then plot a curve showing median amount of salary by years; or, using the index, plot the percentage which the present median salary is of the median 1929 salary. The absolute fall in the one case or the percentage fall in the other would be the measure. The same methods could be used for a study of rise or fall in salary budget as between cities or groups of cities. In the latter study, increase or decrease in school population should not be overlooked. In studies of this type purchasing power of the dollar (or other monetary units) should be held constant.

In such a study several important points of comparison would be worthwhile. For instance: Did American teachers suffer salary reductions relatively earlier or later in the depression than did teachers in Denmark, Italy, Sweden, Brazil, or Mexico? Was there a longer or shorter period in America than in the other countries during which reductions were in effect? At the different stages were the reductions relatively greater or less in Ameri-

---

[12] In the United States such data with median salary given for each type of teacher, by size of city, are published biennially in the *Research Bulletins* of the National Education Association (usually in March of the odd years). These are available as far back as 1923. Since 1933 such figures for rural teachers have been included wherever such material was available by state.

For the latest of these studies see: National Education Association, Research Division. "Salaries of School Employees, 1934-35." Research Bulletin 13: 1-31, March 1935. See also: "Salaries of Elementary Teachers in Europe." *School and Society* 40: 226-28, August 18, 1934. (Quoted from the *Educational Supplement* of the *London Times*.)

ca? In the different countries were reductions in personnel used to effect retrenchment before actual salary reductions were made?

Data for such studies are published in official reports, though their arrangement would not be equally convenient for use in all countries. In foreign countries the statistics required will appear in reports of the chief educational official. Sometimes such statistics are published independently and sometimes in combination with all government statistics.[13]

Other Comparative Studies

In depression experiences touching education there are many points of interest with which to compare the several countries of the world with our own. Have other countries shown any new developments, seemingly resulting from the depression, that correspond with movements such as our adult education, our nursery school, our colleges for unemployed, or our CCC? Are our several channels for federal aid to education through the NYA, PWA, FERA, CWA, WPA, and CCC, paralleled by corresponding channels in other countries? What have organized groups of professional workers in other countries accomplished along the line of the work done by our National Planning Board, our State Planning Boards, the Joint Commission on the Emergency in Education, and the Educational Policies Commission?

What happened to attendance at the different school levels in other countries as compared with ours? How do reduction

---

[13] Two references of value in locating sources are: Abel, James F. *National Ministries of Education.* United States Department of the Interior, Office of Education, Bulletin No. 12 1930

Kandel, I. L. *Educational Yearbook of the International Institute of Teachers College, Columbia University.* New York: Bureau of Publications, Teachers College, Columbia University. Published annually since 1924.

The Review of Educational Research for June 1934 offers a valuable review of the literature on this problem.

of total school expenditures here, compare with like figures for countries in Europe, South America, New Zealand, Canada, or Australia? Has our teachers'-oath legislation any parallel in other republics; in countries with other forms of government? (This latter is not solely a depression phenomenon but seems to have gained rapid headway in this period.) According to data appearing in *Publishers' Weekly,* the publication of professional books dropped very materially during the depression in the United States.[14] How do these figures compare with like figures for other countries? In various countries what has happened to the paid memberships of professional and scientific societies and to subscriptions to professional and technical journals? How do different countries compare in attendance at medical, law, engineering, and teacher training schools when data for each are related to predepression attendance figures?

---

[14] The monograph in this series by Waples, Douglas. *Research Memorandum on Social Aspects of Reading in the Depression,* has many helpful suggestions for research in this field.

Chapter III

Problems in the Theory and Philosophy of Education

H AS our depression experience left its impress upon educational theory and philosophy and, if so, in what ways? These fields are extremely wide. There is little that is basic in the way of ultimate objectives and values in institutional management by which to be guided. What is the function of the federal government, the state, or the county in education? Upon what basis are given facts, groups of facts, or specified activities evaluated as subject matter for a given group of children? How are the merits of student government or of a social program for the school judged? Why is there insistence upon the right to wide freedom in teaching? Upon what basis does progressive education rest? What is the basis of the educational program of the TVA or of the CCC? What criteria established the age limits in compulsory attendance laws? Why are there free schools? Why is the school expected to participate in directing social trends? What motivates the general and specific aims of education?

By such questions one may turn to almost any corner of the field of education and at every point the answer is: to a large extent, on the basis of a certain theory or philosophy of education. What is taught is determined by what values are sought and by the reasoning which assumes that such values will accrue as a result of learning. The assumption that free schools have value for democracy, or that democracy cannot exist without free schools, is treated as if it were an established law in nature.

39

Methodology rests a good deal upon the assumption that certain personality changes result from certain learnings, though if it were asked how much of what elements in personality will be produced by a given amount of learning of algebra, music, or history, there would be no ready answer.

However, there is some relatively exact knowledge. There exist facts in many parts of the field; there are measures of some important relationships; there are some well-established principles. However, when these facts are used, there is a tendency to forget that surface matters often are being dealt with, and that beneath the whole of what is being done there are basic assumptions as to values, or as to how values result from learning, or even as to how the learning occurs.

In selecting subject matter for children such assumptions or postulates are really estimates of subject matter values commonly accepted by everyone. This does not mean that these have been *proved* to be the best possible values, but only that at this time they are *believed* to be. Similarly, when dealing with the problem of federal versus state or local control of education, one is dealing largely with argument, and argument proceeds from foundations assumed to be self evident.

All this is by way of saying that in a large degree education rests upon a foundation that is relative and shifting rather than absolute and fixed. One age or one people place great value upon physical development, political sagacity, social graces, religion, science, or technology. There is training for culture at one time; for social efficiency, character, or personality, at others. Naturally, with such shifts in values presuppositions have to be restated if there is to be logical reasoning. In these changes something happens, not to the logic of previous postulates, but to the postulates themselves. New values rise and old ones fall. In life itself there have been changes that destroyed some values and created others. Scientific discovery may have played a part in these shifts, but mostly new interests were due to new contacts and responsibilities of life.

If values are created and maintained in this way the question then is: What did the depression do to alter individual and group needs and relationships? Recently various units of government have functioned in many new ways. People have an entirely new experiential background for understanding what government means; what charity means. Many, heretofore economically independent, are now on relief. Many who were well educated could not utilize their education to raise, nor even to maintain, their usual standard of living. New social groups have been formed and old ones have been dissipated. Every institution has suffered a severe strain. Many groups have given up certain old activities and taken on new ones, in many cases changing their membership. They are in reality different social forces. Upon how many of the social enterprises and processes, then, do people now look with changed feelings? If people see the state, church, bank, industrial corporation, stock market, bridge club, and the sewing circle differently out of these new experiences, demands on them will be different and they will, therefore, be different.

The school is one of society's important institutions. Its function is to help children and youth find their ways while growing into social responsibilities. If the social changes here alluded to have cut deeply enough, they will have altered the relative importance of the values previously embodied in educational theory and philosophy. If the social structure has been jostled severely by this depression, then obviously an attempt should be made to find whether the foundations of any of the underlying assumptions of education have been revised. Within this field many lines of inquiry suggest themselves.

Problems for Research

1. The Federal Government has developed a new position in education. Has this altered theories of control or support of schools?

2. Tuition charges have been introduced into what before had been free schools. Has anything happened to alter the previously accepted concept of free schools; of public education?

3. Academic freedom has been discussed of late with exceptional frequency and bitterness. Is that principle to be given a new statement? Is teaching to hold a new position in society?

4. Government projects in education such as NYA student aid, the schools of TVA[1] and of CCC, nursery schools, and adult education are called emergency measures. Shall they be dismissed as such, or studied as possible new concepts of the function of education in government?

5. Fads and frills, so called, have been widely discarded. Is society through with the values they assumed to offer, or were the values falsely assumed? Upon what grounds were they chosen for discard?

6. Social science gained a substantial position in the curriculum before the depression. At least a theory had been developed in selection of materials for courses in that field. Has that theory withstood practical application to present life; or better, if subject matter is selected for such courses on the same theory, what new material has the depression produced? In one form this query is concerned with the theory, in the other with the practice, of curriculum making.[2]

7. Recent events have forced statesmen to give serious thought to education. Possibly it has been generations since education was so much a political problem as it has been in this period. There is exceptional occasion, therefore, for considering foundation principles. As they are the ones deciding these matters, the pronouncements of these statesmen should be assembled and analyzed.

8. Sociologists have produced an extensive body of literature in recent years. Much of it deals, either directly or by implication, with social theories. Many analyses of the working of social and economic forces in this depression have been offered. This body of literature, omitting that which is largely childish speculation or flamboyant

---

[1] See: Hart, Joseph K. *Education for an Age of Power: The TVA Poses a Problem.* New York: Harper & Bros. 1935. Pp. 245

[2] See: Curtis, Francis D. "Some Effects of the Depression on the Teaching of Social Science." *School Science and Mathematics* 34: 345-60, April 1934

propaganda, is significant for education. If society is being seen in any new ways, or if new interpretation is being given to social forces, certainly the educational theorist should examine the proposals. A study of this literature for its contribution to a philosophy of education would be worthwhile.

9. Is adult education, as developed under recent federal support, going forward under a new theory? Is the theory upon which education has been developed in the Tennessee Valley project different from that commonly used elsewhere? Like questions must be raised about the theories back of CCC and nursery schools.

10. Shall general or specialized curricula receive the greater emphasis? Has depression emphasized what was already commonly believed— that there is less and less chance that a graduate, either of high school or college, may hope to find employment in a position where specialized training counts most and where general training is not important? Has theory as to the relative worth of general and specialized training been wrong?

11. During these hard times it has been emphasized that too many are being trained for white collar jobs, thereby training the country out of competent craftsmen. If these assertions are based upon observation and statistics, they imply a type of social maladjustment. Public education ought not to end in frustration, either for the individual or for society. Is the theory of whom to train, of how many to train, and of how much to train, designed in terms of ideals and aspirations alone, or does it reckon fully with all the practical facts of life? Is it concerned mainly with the attainment of the externals of high cultural level rather than with how that culture gets its work done? If so, then it conceives of culture as something apart from real life. Possibly the depression unemployment may reveal that the theory of public schools omitted certain social elements that have proved of great importance under stress.

12. The 1935 curriculum stands as a stark reminder of a retrenchment program. Surely it contains no fads or frills. Art, music, health activities, home economics, manual training, physical education, kindergarten, supervision, research, schools for handicapped children, have been emasculated or cast out altogether. Viewed at a little distance the program resembles that of 1880. There was a practical side to the task of reducing these programs; much that was done was likely the best possible. At the same time, it is reason-

able to ask upon what theory of education the present decimated program rests.

13. Should education be expected to produce habits, attitudes, or ability to exercise judgment in the new types of life situations created by the recent depression? For instance, has the depression produced new possibilities of government that the next generation will have to understand? Has it revealed the nature of governmental machinery in a new way by showing that government has tremendous social significance? Will the children now in school need more definite understanding of such terms as conservatism, liberalism, individualism, collectivism, democracy, fascism, communism, capitalism, unemployment, poverty, charity, social security, corporation and labor union? Surely they are to settle for their own society the influence of the social forces these terms suggest. It is not mere knowledge of books, but familiarity with these forces; it is attitudes (intelligently arrived at) that are sought. These are not entirely new needs but they have been pushed into the foreground by the depression and certainly have a new significance. The suggestion here is that the theory of what education is should demand search for some of the new elements with reference to which theory needs constantly to be checked and revised.

These are some of the major questions raised in this field by the depression. They may be settled in many ways. Where there is no knowledge there is more than likely to be guesswork. At many points there will be difference of opinion as to values sought. The questions are not solely ones of fact, but largely ones of interpretation. Statesmen, citizens, and educators will differ in their findings on these questions. Issues are sure to arise. In a democracy such issues should be decided on the basis of wide and careful deliberation.

First, the question should be clear. In some instances a problem in the preceding list involves several questions rather than one. Second, any selected theses will have to be set up to be defended, or one or more hypotheses chosen for testing. Third, in cases which involve deduction, argument, and reasoning, the debate may proceed. On a question of fact, the facts will have to be assembled and analyzed to test the chosen hypothesis. In most of these questions both fact and principle are important. Mainly, they require the assembly and analysis of facts. The following sample problems may serve to point the way for research in this field.

Sample Researches

PROBLEM 1

Has the depression led to the establishment of a federal policy on education?

What the Federal Government has been doing for education during this depression raises many important questions.[3] So far no federal policy for education as such has been announced. Yet, there has been vast expansion of educational activities from this source. Some parts of this appear as donations by the Federal Government; some parts appear as purely incidental contributions to education, the chief aim being to provide work for the unemployed; still others appear to be focused upon the solution of certain social problems. The schools themselves have received little or no recognition directly and some of the educational projects of the government have been handled through other than the usual educational channels.

The educational activities of the Federal Government give the impression that in the case of the early land grants for schools, education has been used as a means through which to accomplish some other thing. The sixteenth section grants for schools were a feature of the federal policy affecting public domain, the purpose being to populate and develop the country. Guaranteed educational opportunities were offered as an inducement to these ends. So it appears that many of the recent federal contributions to education have not been concerned with

---

[3] For further research suggestions on this problem see monograph in this series by Clyde, R. and White, Mary K. *Research Memorandum on Social Aspects of Relief Policies in the Depression,* Chapter IX.

education, as such, but only with the need of the people to be fed and sheltered.

It may well be that there is no federal education policy, but that other federal policies definitely *affect* education. Perhaps this is a negative policy—one that calls for no definite, responsible, or continuous program. However, even a negative policy assumes freedom to use educational activities without regard for the existing public policies by which free schools are maintained. It is one thing for a government to formulate and announce its policy and to guide legislation and administrative procedure by it. It is a different thing to legislate and administer as occasion arises, judging what action to take only when the situation actually is faced. Obviously, governments do both of these and both procedures have their merits. Properly formulated, a policy should provide for diversity of cases and for change. Eventually, however, most policies need complete restatement. To be operating continually in either a legislative or administrative field without a policy of some sort is apt to result in governmental friction and maladministration.

If the Federal Government has no real educational purpose that fits into the generally accepted theory of public education and that expresses itself in ventures that harmonize with the programs set up and managed by states or other responsible political units, then there is urgent need for a study of federal activities in education; the aim of which would be to determine whether the consistency of its acts in this field to date, if carefully analyzed, would provide the basis for a policy. In order to carry out such a study the following activities would require analysis:

1. Federal aid in the form of land grants to the states.[4]

---

[4] For example see: Swift, Fletcher Harper. *Federal and State Policies in Public School Finance.* Boston: Ginn & Co. 1931. Pp. 472

2. Federal aid in the form of money grants to the states.[5]

3. Emergency relief aid during the depression.[6]

It may be assumed that there is a wide enough range of federal experience in education to provide for the working and testing of certain principles. The search would then be for those principles. A good policy would include principles of action in all recent federal legislative and administrative regulations that affect education. The first step would be to assemble these principles from the numerous statutes, court decisions, administrative procedures, presidential orders, and rules covering educational activities. It would then be necessary to determine whether these principles are in harmony with each other, with the older federal acts concerning education, and with state and local educational policy.

The present need for this study is apparent. There is the urgent need for federal participation in school support throughout the country. There is also need to allay the fear which, rightly or wrongly, does exist and is more than ever aroused by recent federal activities, lest the present trend lead to a degree of federal control of education. The people should know what their Federal Government is doing in this field. The more highly centralized government becomes, the greater is the fear of federal control of schools. Moreover, if the Federal Government should give up the principle of checks and balances and allow control to fall into the executive division of the government, this fear would be still greater. Some aspects of this prob-

---

[5] See: Mort, Paul R. *Federal Support for Public Education.* New York: Teachers College, Columbia University. 1936. Pp. 334

[6] See: Studebaker, J. W., U. S. Commissioner of Education. *New Federal Expenditures for Certain Phases of Education from 1933 to the Present Time.* January 1, 1936. Presented for the information of the Educational Policies Commission of the National Education Association. See also: Covert, Timon. *Federal Grants for Education, 1933-34.* U. S. Office of Education, Leaflet No. 45. Washington, D.C.: Government Printing Office, 1935. Pp. 14

lem have been discussed, but no adequate study of it, either as a question of government or as a question of public school policy, has been undertaken.[7]

PROBLEM 2

Has the generally accepted theory of education for all the children of all the people been disturbed by this depression?

Basic education is offered free or practically free of charge to everyone. Parents, scholars, statesmen, and schoolmasters urge every child to go as far as possible in his studies. This is not a passing whim. There is a profound general conviction of the rightness of this idea. If there is such a thing as a general upward surge of the masses in America, universal education is clearly the main avenue through which it expresses itself.

Certain recent statements that there are too many white collar workers and no adequate supply of skilled craftsmen may at first seem out of harmony with the free-school idea. The character and extent of recent unemployment among college graduates raises a fear in some minds lest high aspirations become impossible of realization. Can the trend to raise the cultural level of the people by education be continued without producing too many white collar workers? Can there be abundance of culture without upsetting the adjustment of the people to tasks essential for the maintenance of that cultural level?

[7] For a background see the following: Cubberley, Ellwood P. *State School Administration.* Boston: Houghton Mifflin Co. 1927. Pp. 773

Federal Relations to Education Part I. 744 Jackson Place, Washington, D.C.: National Advisory Committee on Education. 1931

Bryan, William Lowe and Kohlmeier, Albert Ludwig. "Educational Policies of the United States Government," "Federal Aid to Education." *Indiana University Studies,* Vol. XVII, Study No. 87. March 1930

Taylor, Howard Cromwell. *The Educational Significance of the Early Federal Land Ordinances.* New York: Teachers College, Columbia University. 1922. Pp. 138

Thompson, Walter. *Federal Centralization.* New York: Harcourt, Brace & Co. 1923. Pp. 399

It is probable that this aspiration of education for all should continue for centuries in a static civilization, but it may not survive unchallenged in a rapidly changing one. The question of its soundness would be raised whenever serious maladjustment occurred. This depression provided the chance for a piling up of previous strains due to technological developments.

What chance is there for providing jobs for trained people?[8] It should be possible to determine whether the rate of increase in white collar jobs is equal to the rate of output in institutions of higher education. The determination of this fact is of first importance. As matters now stand, one's job is, in general, an accepted index of one's social status and intellectual worth. That is, well educated people feel at a serious social disadvantage (not to mention economic) if they are forced to accept positions on an occupational level lower than that for which they were prepared by education. This relation of educational to occupational levels is a tradition. Back of it has been the assumption that by getting more education one can get a higher type of position. Some may say this is a foolish tradition, but it is clearly an element in the theory of free schools. If there are not enough white collar jobs, then the people are faced with the dilemma of either breaking the tradition or of modifying educational theory.

To break the tradition would require the modification of a set of established values. The proposition might have to be accepted that one cannot expect (except by chance) to hold a job that utilizes the intellectual and cultural equipment possessed or that is implied by the schooling received. The claim that more

---

[8] Of interest here is the following: Amidon, Beulah. "After College—What?" *Survey Graphic* 22: 320-23, June 1933. This is a discussion, with some figures, of the chances for employment after graduation. See also: Chamberlain, Leo M., and Meece, L. E. *The Graduate of the College of Education and the Depression*. Bulletin of the Bureau of School Service, Vol. 6, No. 1. Lexington: University of Kentucky. 1933. Pp. 38

education guarantees a better occupational position might have to be given up. There may be a necessity to find a way of classifying people culturally so as to distinguish cultural level from both occupational and educational levels. Frank facing of these problems is an actual need if society is to go on indefinitely extending its educational ladder.

If this dilemma should be met by giving up the theory of free schools, a way would have to be found to limit training. Would it be done by charging fees, by examinations, or by other means? It is when a practical solution to such questions is sought that it is realized how this theory of free schools is woven into the entire social and political philosophy. To give up this educational theory would require far more social and mental adjustment than is suggested by the seemingly simple question of how to administer a selective scheme. To ask the average American to accept a theory by which he might find himself or his children without a chance to go as far in education as their abilities enabled them would be interpreted as asking him to accept aristocracy as the basis of his society.

There is another possibility that research should not overlook. The fact that there are more workers than jobs in some of the upper classes of occupations might be due to erroneous ideas of education. Such an hypothesis is worth examining. Is it conceivable that there is a need for a large amount of reconstruction within the educational program that would result in focusing education more intelligently upon the problems of life, not only for the individual but for society, and so lead to a far better adjustment between training status and occupational status?[9]

---

[9] See: Coxe, W. W. "The Changing Occupational Pattern in New York State and Its Implications for Education." *Official Report, 1936*. Washington, D.C.: American Educational Research Association, a department of the National Education Association. 1936. Pp. 240-44

See also: Kinney, Lucien B. "Education for Economic Security." *Annals of the American Academy of Political and Social Science* 182: 30-40, November 1935

The somewhat new kinds of education being developed in connection with government relief programs and the increasing evidence of the value of informal post school training call for research along this line.

These problems can be examined, in part, by study of trends in numbers of various types of jobs and numbers of people with various amounts of schooling. Population and occupational statistics of the Bureau of the Census and educational statistics from the Office of Education would provide the starting point. Numerous studies of population and of employment are available to supplement these main sources.

Chapter IV

Problems in Student Personnel

W HAT effect has the depression had upon the school
population? Here school population means all those
eligible under the law to go to school. The concern is not with
individuals but with the group. However, what happens to
pupils individually alters the average status of the entire group.

The Field Covered

What the depression may have done to change this group is
of importance. Did the group grow or decline in size? Did
its social composition change? Did it attend school more or less
regularly than before? Did it shift its choice of studies or its
educational interests? Did it become more critical and recalci-
trant? Did it show greater or less amounts of illness? Did
children of minority groups (e.g., Negroes, Indians) reflect
depression influences in any special ways?[1] Did the age or the
sex distribution of the school population change in any of the
divisions of the school system? Did regularity of attendance rise
or fall throughout the school system? Did attendance at schools
with general programs show greater or less change than that for
technical and professional schools? Did the numbers graduating
from various units and types of schools show any change from
previous trends?

Did the retrenchment plans used for high schools affect the
school privileges of certain groups adversely, while benefiting

---

[1] For a discussion of problems of minority groups see monograph in this
series by Young, Donald. *Research Memorandum on Minority Peoples in the
Depression.*

other groups? Did retrenchment affect schools for atypical children more or less than other schools? Did the school population shift more or less than usual as indicated by transfers from district to district or institution to institution? Did new youth movements appear among college students? Did the colleges receive more or fewer married students during these years? Do retardation statistics show increase or decrease? Did the occupational ambitions of high school and college students change from those for predepression groups?[2] What has become of depression-time graduates from colleges and universities? Did more students work to earn their ways through college than before? Did those who received government aid do as well in school as others?[3] What is the attitude of this group toward government, college, research, marriage,[4] corporations? When more leisure was thrust upon young people suddenly, as in this depression, what part of it, if any, did they tend to use in study?[5] Did output of trained physicians, ministers,[6] teachers, lawyers, engineers, pharmacists, veterinarians, archeologists, keep pace with previous trends? Has the occupational level of employed college graduates changed? How many youths aged 15 to 21 were gainfully employed and how many of this group were in school during this period as compared, say, with 1926? Is the route for a college graduate to a chosen career leading through a number of varied jobs more now than it was in the twenties? What trends do compulsory attendance statistics show for

[2] Nietz, John A. "The Depression and the Social Status of Occupations." *The Elementary School Journal* 35: 454-61, February 1935

[3] Touton, Frank C. "Scholastic Aptitudes and Achievements of FERA Students." *School and Society* 42: 269-71, August 24 1935

[4] See monograph in this series by Stouffer, S. A. and Lazarfeld, Paul F. *Research Memorandum on the Family in the Depression,* Chapter VI.

[5] See monograph in this series by Steiner, Jesse F. *Research Memorandum on Recreation in the Depression.*

[6] See monograph in this series by Kincheloe, Samuel C. *Research Memorandum on Religion in the Depression.*

this period? What legislation during the period affected eligibility for school or requirements for attendance? Was there an unusual number of problems in emotional adjustment? Who are the young people in the CCC camps and why are they not in high school or college? Who are the people attending the many temporary, emergency, or depression colleges? Have student strikes increased in this period, and, if so, what seems to be back of them? What are the attitudes of students in various classifications, toward the depression, and toward the school? Do school people think the school personnel is different in any way from predepression groups?

Need for Research in This Field

Many more such questions as these might be asked. Most of them are important; answers to them would help educational needs to be seen in a new light. There is no more important question for education than that which asks what manner of person it is who seeks aid at the school.

The school population may be affected in two ways, either by changing the students eligible and attending, or by changing what education is to do for the student. This latter means a change in the student's educational aims and aspirations; if the school is keeping pace, it will mean also a changed school. This depression has affected the school population in both of these ways. Direct changes are seen in the numbers of old students returning and in new additions such as the adult school groups. Indirect changes are reflected in the many recent educational projects set up for new kinds of training.

Only by a study of the school population and of the problems it faces is there hope of understanding whether or not the depression has brought to light any new educational needs. Further, it is only by such study that there is gained a sound judgment of the retrenchment policies and plans that have been pursued by school authorities during this period.

The problems suggested here approach education from the standpoint of those who are to be educated—who they are and what their educational needs are, rather than from that of the world they are to live in, from that of organized knowledge, or from that of the school as it stands. The search proposed is for depression effects on the educational needs of the country as these are revealed in changes that have come in the population to be served by organized education.

It has been said that students are far more serious about getting an education than they were before the depression. If some definition of what is meant by "serious," and if some measure of this trait could be worked out, it might reveal a positive effect of the depression that should have permanent worth. If that attitude could be defined and measured, insight as to how to produce a serious purpose in school would be gained. It is said that youth and adults alike, have turned to serious study as a means of solace. Has any educational institution considered such an idea in relation to aims for its studies? At all times, to say nothing of times of disaster, there are thousands of people struggling to regain their hold on life. Frustrations need not always end by leaving their victims in bitter despair. There are many shades and outcomes of discouragement. Education might restore mental balance; a feeling of self-confidence; hope; or the thrill of mastery.

It is said, also, that during this depression secondary school and college students have become much more interested in public affairs, and in government and socio-economic theory; that students are better informed and hold more clearly defined positions on social and political philosophy. There is an assumption that liberalism and even radicalism have gained ground among students. There is said, also, to have developed among a small number of youth a fatalistic attitude which sees no hope and so surrenders.

This field of attitudes is a hazy one for scientific study. But since these young people soon will be in charge of government, industry, and education, there is no doubt as to the importance of their views. Their beliefs are in terms of what they see, know, enjoy, and suffer. It may not matter so much whether they lean politically toward the left or toward the right, but it matters greatly whether they retain their mental balance; whether they become hopeful or despairing.

Method, Techniques, and Sources

In much of this field research should concern relatively simple statistics involving classifying and counting cases. How to classify for study depends upon what one wants to know and whether there is any prospect of getting the necessary facts. There are many questions in this field for which no answers exist in statistical form, and the chance of obtaining them from other sources is slight.

In general there are two types of questions: one dealing with numbers (of students or groups); the other with traits, attitudes, behavior, achievements. In the former case, classification is easier because it has to do with phenomena that are unitary and definite. The latter is concerned with qualities, phases, aspects, characteristics, and attitudes that are not separate but have to be abstracted. Here the data are far less tangible. For the first type there are well established sources of recorded facts and statistical summaries such as state school statistics published biennially by the United States Office of Education; cumulative record cards; special records in pupil-personnel offices; and official reports of local, county, state, and national educational officials. For the second type additional material will be necessary. There is always the possibility of gathering data, by use of questionnaires, directly from the people studied. The value of such data depends upon how they are gathered. Research workers should be alert to distinguish between fact and fancy.

In order to go far with the second type of problems, data

must be newly developed. One cannot determine whether a student is suffering from frustration by asking him directly. The student himself may not know. For meeting this need, testing has come to have large possibilities by extending its territory to cover traits of character and personality as well as intelligence and achievement. Testing for attitudes, feelings of inferiority, loss of morale, and beliefs is already an accomplished fact.[7] This field requires the use of such techniques.

The problems set up for study in the section following indicate how these several types of study apply. They do not illustrate research in all parts of this field.

Sample Researches

PROBLEM 1

In what ways, if at all, did attendance statistics at institutions of higher learning reflect the influence of the depression?

Assuming that cost is one important factor in determining where young people will go to college, then, by way of hypotheses, it would be reasonable to expect: (1) that free-tuition schools would be favored during a prolonged depression; (2) that schools close to home would be favored as opposed to those at a distance; (3) that transfers from high-tuition to low-tuition schools would be in larger numbers than usual; (4) that relatively more students would have applied for government aid in the low-tuition than in the high-tuition schools; (5) that upper division and graduate attendance would decrease more than that for lower divisions; and (6) that perhaps attendance of women would drop more than that for men.

---

[7] The work of the Institute of Child Welfare of the University of Minnesota (see its Monograph Series) is a noteworthy development in this field. For references to pertinent researches consult: Hildreth, Gertrude H. *A Bibliography of Mental Tests and Rating Scales*. New York: Psychological Corporation. 1933; also Vol. II, No. 3, June 1932, and Vol. V, No. 3, June 1935 of *Review of Educational Research*. Washington, D.C.: American Educational Research Association

The importance of a study of this problem is apparent. Tuition is a source of revenue for nearly all institutions of higher learning. In importance it varies widely. The support for higher institutions comes mainly from taxes, endowments, current gifts, and tuitions. In a serious depression all these sources would be affected. Hence, what happens to tuition income as a result of shift in attendance is important.

If hypothesis number one is true, then the depression-attendance figures for most state-supported schools (junior colleges, colleges, universities) should have shown a greater increase over the figures for 1925 to 1929 than those of independent and church schools.

If number two is true, then the student bodies in independent institutions should have become somewhat more local. Those at state or low-tuition schools should have remained constant or even become more cosmopolitan, since students could better afford to travel a little farther to get to a free-tuition school.

If number three is true, then the independent schools must have held relatively smaller percentages of their old students than usual. In a depression some students will still be able to go where they like so far as cost is concerned, while some will be so seriously affected that, without aid, they would not be able to go to any school. It would seem that total attendance at all institutions would be reduced. However, other factors enter. During this depression, although there was little chance for employment, many people believed there would be opportunity in a year or so. This reasoning undoubtedly led many students, particularly in the upper division and graduate schools, to borrow money or otherwise arrange to go to college during the depression years. That is, while ability to pay his own way dropped for the student, the attractiveness of staying at home, or of the chance to get a job, also decreased. Hence, the likelihood of his going to college may have been left somewhere near what it was before. This is not a complete analysis of all factors that might influence attendance, but suggests the lines of reasoning and investigation.

To test out this reasoning would require data for institutions classified according to tuition cost.[8] The data required would include total attendance; attendance by classes, years, and sex; transfers and place from which transfer was made; old students returned; new students that are not transfers; distribution of each group by distances from home; and the numbers applying for government aid.[9] The data might be gathered for 1920 to 1937 and arranged with 1926 as the base.

The extent of this study could be large or small. It would be worth making even though it included only two institutions. Ten institutions would, of course, be more conclusive; forty (provided they were properly selected), still more so. Some of the questions raised might be omitted if data could not be obtained. If a larger number of institutions were included, more types could be represented. What is needed is a thorough study for all types on a scale large enough to provide a basis for understanding fully how young people reacted toward college attendance during a prolonged depression. For data, the registrar's office of the institution in question is the starting point. Student directories, catalogues or registers and sometimes enrollment statistics are issued from this office.[10]

---

[8] A series of tuition studies have been made by U. H. Smith who reports yearly on these trends. The latest is: "Fees in State Educational Institutions." *Minutes of Twenty-Sixth Meeting, 1936.* Appleton, Wisconsin: Association of University and College Business Officers (Sec. R. J. Watts, Lawrence College) 1936. Pp. 33-34

[9] See: National Youth Administration. *The Works Program.* Release No. 6-198. January 1937. Mimeo. This is a detailed report, by states, of numbers of students continuing high school and college through government aid.

[10] Walters, Raymond. "Statistics of Registration in American Universities." *School and Society* 34: 783-96, December 12, 1931; 36: 737-47, December 10, 1932; 38: 781-94, December 16, 1933; 40: 785-801, December 15, 1934; 42:

PROBLEM 2

What has become of the graduates of secondary and higher schools since January 1929?

Numerous writers have referred to the "lost generation." What has happened to those who completed work for the Doctor of Philosophy, the Master of Arts, or the Bachelor of Arts degree? Did society go to the expense of training those people and then allow them to fall by the wayside? What do these young people think of it all? How do they view education, the college, the state, social conventions, law, science, marriage, home and family? What is their present prospect for a chance to achieve as they thought they would when they entered college? All these questions ought to be answered. A nation can hardly afford to have its young people, several years in succession, completely thwarted in life, for that inevitably means a gap in the leadership of the country a few years later.

This broad social question is also an important educational one.[11] In the long run society is apt to think that what one can do with his education is a measure of the worth of the schools that produced it. Society is likely to support education accordingly. Schools can do nothing better than to study the successes and failures of their students.

To study this problem a count would need to be made of all graduates, by groups and by types of courses pursued. Further analysis by sex, age, marital status, basis of support in school and after graduation, father's occupation, and occupational purposes and experiences would be pertinent. Did the technically

801-10, December 14, 1935. Probably continuing annually. Also, Wilkins, Ernest H. "Major Trends in Collegiate Enrollments." *School and Society* 42: 442-48, September 28, 1935

[11] Chamberlain, Leo M. and Meece, L. E. "The Graduate of the College of Education and the Depression." *Bulletin of the Bureau of School Service.* Lexington, Kentucky: College of Education, University of Kentucky. Vol. VI, No. 1. September 1933

and professionally trained students fare differently from those who followed general courses? Of each of these groups and sub-groups, how many obtained jobs at once upon graduation, a year later, two years later, three years later, or not at all? Of those who did not get jobs, how many returned to school; how many remained at home; how many went away from home? Of those who obtained employment, how many of each group found the kind of position for which they were trained? If not, did the kind of position hold any relation to the training or represent a level of work at all in line with the amount of training? Again, of those obtaining work, how temporary or permanent was each job?

In such a study special note should be taken of the relative chances of unemployed graduates of one or more years' standing and present classes of graduates. Are members of the new classes being chosen in preference to the older candidates? If so, what appears to be the explanation?

If such a study were undertaken on any except an institutional scale it probably would have to be handled through the personnel divisions of the schools. As follow-up service is limited in most institutions, one could hardly hope to find adequate records available. The data might be gathered for large enough samples of graduates to provide a sound basis for evaluating the effects of the depression at this particular point. A suitable form for checking and a suitable covering letter, sent out under the auspices of the *alma mater,* ought to produce large returns. It is the kind of research that should start as part of the work of the student-personnel service in every institution. One phase of this research done in a scientific way is well illustrated by a recent study of depression attitudes.[12] Seven separate tests or scales were devised and administered to some 3,000 adolescents

[12] Rundquist, Edward A., and Sletto, Raymond F. *Personality in the Depression: A Study in the Measurement of Attitudes.* Minneapolis: the University of Minnesota Press. 1935. Pp. 398

of both sexes, some of whom had suffered in the depression and some of whom had not. The analysis of findings by the authors leaves little doubt as to the significance of depressions for personality changes. With this work done, there seems little doubt that suitable tests could be devised for the study here proposed. With the population so widely scattered it would be difficult to get the data, but once gathered the worth of it might easily warrant the expense.

The facts about what has happened to this important group of people is one study. Where they have been and what they have done, compared with what people in the same age groups formerly have done and with what they had prepared to do, is another study. What they think of it all; what it has done to their attitudes, beliefs, self-confidence, ambitions, is yet another study.

PROBLEM 3

Who makes up the population attending the various emergency, unemployed or depression colleges?

It is reasonable to assume that there is some special explanation of the new types of higher education. If they are strictly depression phenomena, then they may disappear in time (to return, perhaps, with other depressions). If they have other elements in them, they should be studied seriously. The hypothesis that part of the student personnel in these institutions is suffering from frustration produced by the depression would provide a point of attack.

By depression college is meant the special colleges (or junior colleges) or branches of schools that were organized and operated for the unemployed during the depression.[13] A study of

[13] There have been many of these. Possibly they have revealed an unmet educational need of some importance. Those at Lafayette, Indiana; Fort Royal, Virginia; Yonkers, and White Plains, New York are illustrations. Corresponding

this movement in all its aspects would add a valuable section to American educational history. Only a small part of this broad study is here proposed, viz., who are the people that make up the student body of this new venture in higher education?[14] Why did this sort of activity appeal to them? What are the wants that are being satisfied?[15]

It may be assumed that many students do not know just why they enjoy such activity or could not easily explain if they knew. Some, no doubt, would not admit all the reasons. This means that, while data may be obtained in part by direct inquiry, some of the facts will have to be discovered by other means.

There are several parts to the problem. First, how many such students are there and where do they live? Second, what are their physical and social traits? Third, what kind and amount of training have they had; when did they have it; and how has it related to their careers? Fourth, what are their present intellectual interests (e.g., is the present study being pursued with a view to improving economic status, to changing occupations, to satisfying desire for a degree, to satisfying intellectual ambition or appetite, or because it is entertaining and provides something to do that others are doing)? Fifth, what has been their experience as wage earners?[16]

A common technique for getting these facts would be by interview, using a printed form designed for the purpose. While much data of value would be obtained if the student were given

---

types of junior colleges were established in Michigan, Ohio, New Jersey, and Connecticut.

[14] See Lide, Edwin S. "The Social Composition of the CWES Junior College in Chicago." *School Review* 43: January 1935. Pp. 28-33

[15] See: Pressey, S. L. "Outstanding Problems of Emergency Junior College Students." *School and Society* 43: 743-47, May 30, 1936

[16] As an example see: Burdell, Edwin S. "An Adventure in Education for the Unemployed." *Ohio State University Emergency School*. Ohio State University. 1933. Pp. 47. This is a complete analysis of 400 students enrolled for a six-weeks' course—their economic background, age and other personal information, and their problems.

the form to fill out and return at his convenience, that is a poor way in comparison with that of having groups fill out the form in the presence of the research worker.

Beyond this wide variety of fact, descriptive of these students, it would be important to know who they are from the standpoint of their intellectual abilities and their attitudes toward life. What do they think of the depression, of what the government has done about it; of their own experiences in suffering loss or in helping others to bear loss; of liberal versus conservative government? Their attitudes toward capitalism, communism and socialism, toward war, peace, public education, marriage and children might be studied.

What one would get as reactions to direct questions on those points might be valuable but likely the test technique mentioned in the previous question would be far more adequate at points.

PROBLEM 4

What have been the effects of the depression on school attendance in general?

The number of persons enrolled in schools has been increasing in recent years. There are a number of sources of data on school attendance. These include record cards, special records in personnel offices, and official reports of local, county, state and national educational officials. As the reliability of these records is not always high nor uniform, there is ample room for research also into the adequacies of the source materials.

The increase in the number of students at various types of schools during the depression years is not necessarily a satisfactory index, however, of the effects of the depression on school attendance. For one thing, it is conceivable that the increase might represent, in whole or in part, the continuation of a long time upward trend in the number of persons attending school. For another thing, it should be remembered that the number of persons attending school is, to a considerable extent, a function of the age composition of the population. Furthermore, the depression may have had differential effects on the school attendance of different sectors of the population when considered by age; sex; nativity; race; economic status; religion; place of residence (urban-rural, city size, region); and type of school (elementary, high school, college, special schools, public, private, parochial, etc.). Studies of the effects of the depression on school attendance therefore should attempt to control the age composition of the population, to eliminate the secular trend, and to get at differential effects by as many of the factors enumerated above as can be controlled.

The importance of controlling the age composition of the population and eliminating secular trend in studies of school attendance cannot be overemphasized. As a sample, the Biennial Surveys of the United States Office of Education were used in order to secure data by school years from 1919 to 1936. The percentage of population aged 14 to 17 years attending high school in each year since 1920 was estimated from the total number in public high schools and the total population aged 14 to 17 years. These latter data were estimated by interpolation of ratios of population 14-17 years of age to total population between 1920 and 1930, and extrapolation to 1937. Population was estimated as of January 1 of each year.

The number of students enrolled in high school in the United States underwent three distinct stages of growth during the period from 1919 to 1936. In the period from 1919 to 1925, that of most rapid growth, the average annual rate of increase was 10.3 per cent.[17] From 1927 to 1929 the average annual rate of increase in high school enrollees slowed down to 3.9 per cent. During the depression years for which data are available, 1931 to 1936, this average annual rate increased to 5.9 per cent. If, however, the growth of the population is examined, it is dis-

---

[17] Calculations are based on biennial data for school years beginning in 1919 from *Biennial Survey of Education.*

covered that the average rates of annual increase in the number of persons 14 to 17 years of age, from which high school students are largely drawn, were, for the same periods, 1.9, 1.6, and .9 per cent. Thus, it is clear, even from this cursory observation, that a portion of the increase in high school enrollment is attributable to the increase in the size of the potential high school population.

If the age composition of the population is held constant by studying the changes in the percentage of the total population of high school age which is actually enrolled, the average annual rate of increase for the first period is 7.7 per cent as contrasted with 10.3; for the second period, 2.3, as compared with 3.9; and for the depression period 4.3, as against 5.9.

Finally, to gauge the effects of the depression on high school enrollment a study should be made of the extent to which such enrollment increased more rapidly during the depression years than would be expected if the "normal rate of increase" were constant. "Normal" for purposes of this illustration could be defined as the trend during the period from 1920 to 1929.

Detailed studies of this type aiming at total and differential effects, may be possible in a number of states and localities. Attendance data are generally available and these can be related to the United States Census or, where available, to local school or other census data. Population censuses of varying scope have been taken during the depression under the auspices of the Civil Works Administration, the Federal Emergency Relief Administration, and the Works Progress Administration in several states, as well as in many of the larger cities. Moreover, some of these censuses have inquiries on school attendance, the analysis of which may contribute valuable information. Data should be obtained for a long-time period if possible, particularly because of the disturbing influence of the war years.

Attempts should also be made to study school attendance during the recovery period. It would be interesting to ascertain whether school attendance will show a relatively permanent depression effect, that is, whether enrollment will maintain the high levels of the depression years; whether recovery will result in a return to the "normal" expectation in attendance; or whether it will result in a drop to levels below the pre-depression years. Such studies can be based on techniques similar to those discussed above.[18]

OTHER PROBLEMS

Research is needed on a large scale to determine, if possible, what the school population of this country really ought to include. The school population has grown steadily for many years and during this depression has shown a further startling expansion. The relation of this growth to unemployment seems obvious, but why did so many turn to study and why did the government institute such projects as CCC, the nursery school, the adult education program, the NYA, and its student relief program? Why have so many depression colleges sprung up? How many and what per cent of the population were required to do the nation's work in 1880, in 1900, in 1920 and in 1936[19] There is far more leisure now than in 1880 and the trend appears to be toward still more. Is there a trend by which could be predicted roughly the number of workers of all sorts needed a decade hence? While this is a problem for sociologists and economists, education is automatically involved. If the percentage of the population needed for work could be established then it would be necessary to raise certain other questions. Suppose it were decided that the 24 to 55 year-olds would furnish

[18] For further suggestions or techniques see Burgess, W. Randolph. *Trends in School Costs.* New York: Russell Sage Foundation, 1920. Carr, William G. *School Finance.* Stanford University Press, 1933. Chapter I.

[19] Of interest here will be: Hurlin, Ralph G., and Givens, Meredith B. "Shifting Occupational Patterns." *Recent Social Trends in the United States.* Report of the President's Research Committee. New York: McGraw-Hill Co. 1933. Pp. 268-324

a force large enough to do the world's work and yet provide reasonable work load and ample vacation. Then, what about those younger and older? For these must be thought out a constructive program. Education will clearly be one feature of this program. The very young will be cared for by parents; the aged by some form of social security. Is the remaining group to be entirely a school population, or could some other activity be injected to absorb part of this leisure? Would so much leisure tend to stimulate here the European type of military training program? Shall one element in the program of the work group be some forms of education and recreation? What might education do to develop interests that consume some of this leisure?[20] This is a stimulating line of inquiry.

There are many more thought-provoking questions at the beginning of this chapter. The question of how to prepare and enter a career grimly stares young people in the face, and makes of them quite different students than they were before. Most of the queries raised in this chapter are but one side of the school's problem. If the depression has changed students it has thereby set new problems for the school itself. The child's problem at once becomes a curriculum, a management, a method, a building, a finance problem for the school to solve. These other sides are the concern of other chapters.

---

[20] See: Lies, Eugene T. *The New Leisure Challenges the Schools.* Washington, D.C.: Published by the National Education Association for the National Recreation Association, 1933. Pp. 326

Chapter V

Problems in the
Program of Instruction

WHAT should children be experiencing at school? The depression has provoked this question anew. The old question was: What subjects shall the school teach? It was put in that way because school subjects were matters of long tradition and were highly respectable, both in age and supposed virtue. The question is stated differently now because more importance is attached to the student and less to the school subject as such.

Depression and Curriculum

This suggests an approach to research in this field. If subjects have value irrespective of the life one lives, then there would be no point in asking what effect the depression had upon the curriculum, for the effect would be nil. If the value of certain subjects does depend upon the life to be pursued by the learner, then the depression may have had a profound effect on those subjects.

Changes may have come to students directly; they may have come to the institutions, the social conventions and proprieties; or they may have come to the economic processes and techniques within life's limitations. Formerly, it was assumed that school subjects, school disciplines, would fit the student to meet this changed world. Now, the assumption is that he should explore his way amidst these changes, dealing with them as directly as possible and be allowed to build for himself a system of thought, feeling, and understanding. It is on the basis of this

69

latter view only that the kind of research here considered could hope to contribute to an understanding of how the instructional program of the school may have been thrown out of balance, or given new meaning because of the depression.

How Depression Changes May Affect the Educational Program

With this theory of the curriculum it is apparent that an instructional program is essentially individualistic; that whatever changes the essential processes of life automatically changes the ends toward which one travels in education; that is, it changes the stuff of which one builds his world, and so, changes the curriculum. However, the things the child can deal with at school are limited by time, by his degree of mastery of the tools of learning, and by his native capacity as well as by the kind of life he may be expected to lead.

There are really two basic questions. Did the depression alter the group to be provided for, either its members individually or the membership of the group? Did the depression change the social, economic, or physical world in a way that warrants alteration of the instructional program? The first question has been treated in part in Chapter IV. Naturally, with an altered population there will be new aims and corresponding new activities to be experienced or learned at school.

But, besides providing a host of new people seeking education, the depression has no doubt altered the outlook and the meaning of life for many of the students attending before. This altered outlook may be due, not alone to direct depression effects, such as impaired health, changed social and economic status, and altered mode of life, but also to changes in the social world in which the student is to live. Thus, there are new groups to provide for; there are old groups with altered viewpoints; there is a changed world for all. Research is not needed to establish the general fact that there is a large new school population, but it is needed to show how old students have developed new points of view that should be recognized in shaping their educational programs. Thousands of young people have had the experience of being hungry; of being sick and unable to have proper medical care; of receiving charity; of helping other needy people; of living under difficult, crowded conditions; of having no spending money; of seeing parents desperately worried; of seeing hundreds stand in bread lines. How much of this each child has felt and what the experience did to the viewpoint of each may well be a problem for physicians, psychologists, and psychiatrists. But it is safe to conclude that it changed these young people.

As to whether society was changed there is clear evidence. Surely government has changed; the economic structure has changed. Surely many of society's customs, traditions, and conventions have changed. To analyze and define the extent and character of these changes requires research some of which has been proposed in the other monographs of this series.

For education the problem is to interpret these changes for their bearing upon the program of instruction in schools or of education outside of schools. Data for this field, therefore, are social and psychological facts having to do with the student and the social order. The data of mathematics, history, or spelling as subjects of study, could not be affected by a depression. For instructional purposes, however, their value lies in the way they function in the learner's program rather than in the way they function in the logical systems of human knowledge. Research here, then, is concerned first with the educational needs of the people, then with how to satisfy them.

Instructional programs before the depression represented an interpretation of social and psychological data. Beyond affecting the educational needs of the people, the depression may have altered the worth of the program previously in operation. So research may approach this field either from the view of educational needs, or from that of means used to satisfy those needs.

Outline of the Field

Major areas of this field are suggested by the following questions:

1. What effect did the depression have upon the instructional program as it was operating?

2. Did the depression bring to light any especially strong or weak points in the program?

3. What effect, if any, did the depression have upon the educational needs of the country?

4. Did the depression create or reveal any new educational needs for which instructional programs ought to be designed?

Facts that provoke these questions are easily at hand. The first question recalls the retrenchments that eliminated art, music, household arts, the health program, physical training, and other activities from many schools. The second is a reminder of the maladjustment between what young people trained for and what they have been able to do with their training; and of the shift toward general, as opposed to specialized, training. The third question has impressed itself by the changes that have come regarding social and economic trends. The school had not clearly sensed the larger amount of leisure there was likely to be, the fallibility of economic systems, the poor adjustment of training to the possible careers ahead. The last question is raised by the fact that the depression seems to have created new adult education needs, new needs in the nursery school field, in the secondary school field. At least programs have been established in these important fields which are new in the fundamental needs back of them.

Within each of these areas many subordinate questions may be raised.

As regards depression effects on the existing program it may be asked: What studies were dropped by way of retrenchment?

When was each dropped? What studies were combined with others, or abbreviated? Did this happen in all schools alike or differently in large and small systems, in rural and city systems, and in different states? What subject combinations were effected during the depression (such as combining the social sciences)? Was this an economy measure? If it was a loss, can the loss to pupils who have missed one, two, or three years of school work in any one of the eliminated subjects be defined? Was there gain in other subjects while these eliminations were in effect? When the eliminations were effected, for whom was the remaining program designed? Did the elimination penalize all students alike or did it leave a school much better for some social classes than for others? For instance, did high schools eliminate college preparatory courses, or mostly courses of a terminal sort? Taking account only of subject matter covered, how do depression-trimmed programs compare with those in vogue in 1890? In general, were newly developed subjects and activities eliminated, that is, the really modern expressions of present theory of education? Were the old long established formal subjects retained? Was this sound retrenchment for the 1930's? Has there been any shift in the earlier trend favoring terminal courses in the junior-college program? What became of the curriculum-revision movement? What did the depression do to school libraries and to laboratory and play ground equipment? One could pursue most of these questions in the college, high school or kindergarten field almost equally well. They could be turned slightly and fitted into the social-activities program of high school and college. What happened to student government; to student organizations? On the administrative side, many equally pertinent questions are reserved for later chapters.

Under question two above other questions can be raised. Do the unemployment figures argue for or against recent proposals favoring more general and less specialized training? Did the failure of graduates to get jobs indicate that they had been taught less than the truth about training for careers? Has the uncertainty of the permanence of social forms, institutions, customs, conventions, and proprieties been taught directly enough? Has the depression given young people a real grasp of what it means to possess leisure time in a civilization, and of the responsibility for planning to use it? Seeing now that there must be some social planning if our present cultural level is to be maintained, where in the curriculum is this kind of training to be provided? Does the present program give adequate attention to such social conditions and concepts as unemployment, poverty, charity, government relief, conservatism, radicalism, maintenance of social morale, consumer economy, tenantry, thrift, over-production, under-consumption, and old-age security? Has there been adequate training against bad investment methods, high pressure salesmen, false advertising, avenues through which disaster came to many in this depression? On the other hand, if one should assemble the important forces that have proved useful in depression times as well as before, what of the existing morals and manners; what of the virtues would he find listed? Are not the good things still good to teach because they have value by common acceptance of all? A search for traditions, customs, conventions, and proprieties that have been dropped or changed by force of our depression experience similarly would be worth making.[1] Offhand observation leads one to think that much of these have survived. These questions touch not only the content of the instructional program (the experience available to students) but educational objectives as well.

For the third question above, one would ask much the same

---

[1] For an example of setup and procedure here it will be of interest to read: Hart, Hornell. "Changing Social Attitudes and Interests." *Recent Social Trends in the United States.* Report of the President's Research Committee. New York: McGraw-Hill Co. 1933. Pp. 382-442

questions as in number two, but would focus upon educational needs instead of upon what was offered in courses. If the depression seriously altered the economic status of large numbers; if it started our government to doing a long list of entirely new things; if it broke up many old social and business groups; if it caused numbers of new groups to form; if it threw new light upon such accepted practices as thrift and strict conformity to social forms, and even upon morality—then it is not too much to assume that this is a changed world where things have different meanings. Then the aims or objectives of education need restatement; the facts and activities that have been used in the past will need re-sorting in the light of the new meanings they have assumed and in the light of the altered goals and processes of society. There is need to consider what principles and facts of politics, of economics, of history, of art, of music, of mathematics; what skills in the art of living happily and fully, in the art of keeping healthy, in manipulating facts and principles, in managing social and business enterprises, in bodily, conversational and manipulative expression, and in the fabrication of materials this new world needs. The chances are that some of the old materials and skills, attitudes and organizations are less useful now, or at least need a new setting. The old intellectual tools will still be needed but their use and the ways of using them to best advantage may have been altered by the social changes brought about by the depression.

In the field of character and personality development, production of which was once attempted by moralizing, by teaching morals and manners, and which is now attempted as an aspect of the entire regimen of the school, there are many questions. If the virtues sought were listed, the list likely would be much as it was years ago. The ways in which these virtues are expressed, however, would be different. A list of moral "don'ts" for 1890 and 1937 set side by side would likely show many changes. Although the depression did not produce all of them, it is probable that it has produced some important ones. For one study it might be well to plan as complete a list as possible, including old as well as recent interpretations, and find out how certain groups of young people (those from homes on relief and those from homes that suffered little, for example) react to them. Similar studies of taste, manners, and social proprieties would be useful. The opposite attack of getting a picture of what constitutes a sound and wholesome expression of morals and social conventions would be worth trying.

In this same way the field of government needs working over; society's minor and major problems such as unemployment, poverty, government relief, social security, and war need to be re-examined as government activities and checked against earlier practices. The field of economics as it applies in business, government, home management, investment, taxation, international financing, surely needs restudy.

Finally, question four, above, asks whether the depression revealed new educational needs previously not existing or at least not provided. This suggests extensive study of the new programs. For example, the CCC scheme of instruction is here with two astonishing new programs, one a residence program, the other a correspondence program. Also important are the nursery-school development and as a phase of adult education, the newly born colleges for the unemployed. There is the work going on under the Resettlement Administration, the TVA, and the wide application of student aid through the NYA. All these new movements are, in part at least, attempts to satisfy needs that came to light in this depression. There should be studies both of why people wanted such programs and of the programs themselves. What are the students trying to get? What are the programs offering?

As research is reviewed in this field it must be realized that the real task is to analyze the effects of the depression upon social life in a way that will reveal needed change in objectives and in the knowledges, skills, attitudes, experiences, to be provided for in instructional programs.

The types of problems available for study in this field are, therefore, wide, and the limited illustrations offered below leave ample room for the use of imagination beyond the suggestions presented.

PROBLEM 1

Has this depression revealed a large social, political, and economic illiteracy?

The depression has revealed many evidences, among adults and children alike, of social, political and economic illiteracy. This is an important concern of the school curriculum. If significant forces are at work in society about which there is ignorance; if the facts pertaining to the nature, behavior, and effects of these forces are not being studied; if there are social principles of long established merit which are being set aside; and if the school is doing little or nothing about these things, then the social science curriculum is in need of revision. It is not assumed this situation is an entirely new problem. It is clear, however, that the depression has thrown it into new and startling relief. Such a problem could be approached from several angles:

1. Tests might be developed and applied to determine the nature and the extent of socio-economic illiteracy among the different groups.

2. A study could be made of the social, political, and economic facts and principles that have come into new prominence in this depression, checking these against present textbooks, syllabi, and curricula. Discrepancies may fairly be regarded as indicating areas in which young people are socially illiterate so far as formal schooling is concerned.

3. One could start with the textbooks, syllabi, and curricula used in courses which are supposed to provide social training and then check their facts, principles, and interpretations for accuracy and adequacy as judged by their inclusion or omission of current social material.

Here might be three distinct ways of testing the proposal that this depression has so altered social forms, processes, and values that it has left large areas of social illiteracy for which present curricula are inadequate.

The first and second of these would require the assembly of all the new facts and principles that reveal the meanings this depression has had for society. For the first study these materials would be built into a test; for the second or curriculum study they would be worked into a check list against which the curriculum and textbooks would be scrutinized. The third approach would first construct a check list of what textbooks and curricula provide. This would then be checked for the knowledge required to understand society today.

The difficult task would be to find materials. What is it about social life that people do not know and what has become so important in this depression period? A way must be found to isolate these facts and principles. Where are they? In a sense they are attached to social problems and to theories and machinery for reacting to these problems. One plan for carrying out such an analysis might be:

1. List problems that have presented themselves. These could then be classified, probably, in several ways—as political, economic and social; or, as related to occupations, poverty, charity, crime, health, domestic relations, education, recreation, taxation.[2]

2. After classifying the problems, the next step would be to consider how they are being met. By what agency or action? Is it through government, by philanthropy, or by every-fellow-for-himself?

3. The next concern would be with the machinery of government and philanthropy. Here the new features would attach to the new problems and so reveal the nature of the new social machinery and its working.

To get at principles as well as facts, as the analysis proceeds, attention would be focused upon the social, economic and politi-

---

[2] For examples see: Judd, Charles H. *Problems of Education in the United States.* New York: McGraw-Hill Co. 1933. Pp. 214

cal theories involved. One is not socially literate when he knows only the names of the various parts of the social structure; he must know also its purposes and the processes through which it operates.

Obviously, a competent student of the social sciences would be required for a study of this type if it were carried very far. Such a study would keep attention focused upon the question of what constitutes social literacy in this age and society. A standard, or pattern, or norm by which to determine this can hardly be claimed to exist. The educational question, therefore, is to get together the social material that should be understood by all and to arrange it in some order so that it may become a suitable interest of children from the time they enter school until they leave it. No recent years have produced so much new material for this purpose as have the depression years. The problem seems so vast as to be beyond solution. Yet, we have no alternative but to attempt a solution.

The sources for this study would be widely scattered. Local, state, and Federal Government documents, such as statutes and official reports, would provide facts pertaining to government; various yearbooks of scientific societies, treatises and researches in the social sciences, and the newspapers and journals of public opinion provide contacts with what is really vital as fact or principle in the social life.

PROBLEM 2

What should schools offer by way of subject matter (facts, principles, attitudes, methods of studying such phenomena, activities) covering the depression?

Social science teaching could treat this depression episode in an incidental way as it dealt with recent history, with political science, with sociology, with current events. If it did so, it might fail to fit the student to live through the next depression intelligently. On the other hand, it might bring facts and principles of social, political and economic science to bear, merely by way of explaining this very remarkable experience just passed. The preparation of an instructional program covering this incident would require studies to sort out the needed materials.

The importance of having youth really understand this bit of American experience is assumed. It is assumed, also, that it is possible to provide a suitable learning experience covering it. To develop such a program requires the assembly of facts, not facts to be offered as such, but as the means of revealing the problems the people had to face. This search for problems, and not merely the learning of what problems existed, is the experience the young people should get—this on the theory that only by assembling and analyzing the facts can any one of these problems be understood. The search then, is for a *method of study and investigation* through which young people may be guided by their teachers; and the goal of which is the *experience of discovering* the important social problems left by the depression.

If teachers are to point the way, they themselves must know it well. They must first know the problems and work out a procedure for each one by which a young mind may find its way from its own interests and limited knowledge through the masses of fact that reveal the problem. These both concern the curriculum, though the latter is also a problem of teaching method. The student should have the experience of seeking and discovering these problems. Such an experience can start only when the student has before him a really challenging question. Although a student may be troubled over a broad general question, yet before any profitable search for facts can begin, the question must be made clear and specific. It may be assumed that virtually all young people have, or can quickly develop, interests in the depression and its effects, from which they may be launched upon a search for the greater social problems that lie back of the lesser ones.

This search for suitable learning activities would require, first, a study of the contacts young people had with the depression. Considerable data are to be secured from statistical sources, but these should be supplemented by experiences of the students themselves. The latter must often be discovered in discussions. In this task, both teacher and student are inquirers. The teacher knows the problems but searches for the student's interests in them and for the normal process by which the student finds his way from isolated interests and facts to the implications of the facts for the large social problems.

In a sense this involves a plan for teaching rather than for research. Perhaps it is already known that what is proposed can be accomplished. Yet, in another sense it is research. If by this method of study, it can be shown that a class can be led through the process of unraveling, classifying and interpreting masses of fact pertaining to the aspects and episodes of a depression, there should be convincing evidence that there is something better in social science teaching than merely memorizing facts.

PROBLEM 3

Has the depression produced new issues or sharpened old issues that should make them an essential part of the social science curriculum?

This is a question of fact. The answer should not be merely affirmative or negative; it should reveal what new and what old issues seem now to constitute legitimate and important materials for study in secondary school and college. Whether or not the depression has speeded up developments in this matter, discussions within the educational profession indicate that the problem is becoming more acute.

The hypothesis could be either: (1) that the depression has stimulated the development of social issues; or (2) that the former trend in the development of issues has continued unchanged by the depression. It is obvious that the movement should be studied further back than the 1930's, as a means of seeing what forces were at work previous to the depression. The World War was prolific in producing issues. Almost every state or national election produces a few. Issues may arise and be discussed in the press and in the public forums, but because of tradition and an older educational philosophy, never appear as curriculum or teaching problems. Current philosophy of education does not regard the school as an agency for conserving past culture alone, but holds it responsible for helping to shape the social trend as well. This theory makes it mandatory that society's issues be dealt with in school. Naturally, problems or issues must be treated, not in isolation alone, but as expressions of social forces. As this latter view has grown among teachers, issues have begun to flow into the classroom for treatment. It is one thing to have issues and another to permit them to appear in schools. Some thought should be given, therefore, to the question of when issues were first permitted to be dealt with in class. This might well be a separate study. At any rate, it is a factor in determining whether education needs to be or can be concerned with this question.

Steps in the research to locate the issues would call, first, for a definition of what constitutes an issue; second, for locating the sources where social issues are regularly presented; and third, for gathering from these sources careful statements of the issues. Having thus assembled the raw data, the next task would be to classify the issues as political, economic, social, religious, educational, moral or other; and finally, to arrange them in an order suitable for checking against the instructional aims of social science courses.

Research parallel to this ought to be carried out to determine what issues actually are being treated in our present courses. This could be a simple study by questions submitted to teachers of social science subjects. The inquiry also should attempt to determine what the issues are; in what connection they are brought into the courses; how they are treated; the time given to them; the techniques used to safeguard absolute fairness to both sides; and finally, teachers' opinions of the educational worth of their inclusion in school work. This problem is pertinent here, regardless of whether the issues had their origin in the poverty, unemployment and distress produced by the depression, or in other earlier forces. Certainly, when unemployment is large enough economic issues must arise.

If by these studies a list of the important issues, and a list of the issues treated in classes could be produced, together with a full description of the methods used in the latter, it could then be possible to make an experimental study of the entire problem of instruction concerning issues. These are three divisions of one large research project that would produce some definite conclusions as to how to handle controversial issues in class instruction.

This problem is related to that of academic freedom. Many accept it; many oppose it. Of those who accept it theoretically, many deny it practical expression because they believe it cannot be applied without abuse. The philosophy of education under which the school participates in directing the social trend is itself an issue to some extent both among teachers and among thoughtful citizens. To deny to a teacher who believes in the philosophy of education just stated the right to treat controversial matters is to deny freedom in teaching. (See problem 4 in Chapter VI).

PROBLEM 4

What was the effect of the depression on the courses offered?

Studies of the effects of the depression on courses *offered* should be possible in many states and localities. Here, as in the other fields of study suggested, an effort should be made to get at differential effects by type of school and by type of community. For community controls such factors should be considered as: city size; urban-rural character of the community; regional location; economic base (type of industry etc.) ; economic level (median rental, income tax data); severity of the depression (payroll data, unemployment, employment indexes, incidence of relief); and the nativity and race composition of the population.

Data should be collected and compiled on the courses offered over a period of time (e.g. from 1900 to date) for a given sample of schools. It is important that the schools sampled be identical for each year included in the study. From such materials a table could be constructed giving years, by courses of instruction.

The list of courses included could be condensed into some kind of meaningful classification.[3] For college curricula, for example, the following condensed classification might be used:

Social Sciences	Philosophy
Economics	Art and Music
History	
Political Science	*Physical Sciences*
Sociology	
Education	Chemistry
Other Social Sciences	Mathematics
	Physics
Humanities	Others
Language	
English	*Biological Sciences*
French	
German	Psychology
Others	Others

Although it would be highly desirable to have annual data for the entire period studied, it may be necessary, for practical reasons, to use five- or ten-year intervals for the earlier period and annual or biennial data for this depression period.

Here again, in order to gauge the influence of the depression on courses offered it is first necessary to control the secular trend. This can be achieved by projecting the trend for each course

[3] See: Judd, Charles H. "Education." *Recent Social Trends in the United States.* Vol. I. New York: McGraw-Hill Co. 1933. Pp. 331-39

or major division and measuring the difference between such an extrapolation and the actual depression incidence of courses offered.

PROBLEM 5

What was the effect of the depression on the courses taken?

Studies of the effects of the depression on courses *taken* may be of two types. First, studies can be made for given samples of schools, of proportionate student enrollment by courses of instruction offered. Such investigations could follow the methods described above and would reveal the effects of the depression on actual proportionate student enrollment.[4]

Such investigations, however, would not reveal the changing interests of students because of failure to control changing curricula. Studies, in which curricula changes are controlled, could be made in individual schools or samples of schools with: (a) little or no curricular change; or (b) with controlled curricula changes.

It may be difficult to locate schools with no changes or few changes in curricula, although this may be possible if the period studied is sufficiently restricted. The narrowing of the time period rapidly reaches a limit, however, because of the necessity of establishing trends. The latter type of study in which curricula change is controlled is probably more feasible. It should be possible, for example, to study schools with similar curricula changes and to measure the direction of student enrollment as courses offered are restricted, expanded, or changed.

It is clear that controls of this type would to some extent indicate the changing character of student interests. Even if it should prove to be impractical to study a number of schools by

---

[4] The proportion of students enrolled in the various courses of instruction rather than absolute numbers should be used. This would control the trend in total student enrollment. Studies can, of course, be made of the trend in absolute numbers as well.

this method, studies of individual schools which indicate the direction of student enrollment within the range of courses offered, may prove fruitful and significant if made for a sufficient number of individual schools. Such studies, for example, should make it possible to answer questions such as: Did students interests shift to the social sciences (or to economics) during the depression?

Still a further refinement can be introduced by studying proportionate enrollment in elective courses in high schools and colleges or through the study of departments of specialization—"minors" and "majors."

Chapter VI

Problems in Staff Personnel

RESEARCH in the field of depression effects upon the teacher personnel is of supreme importance. Whatever happens to stimulate or to distract teachers is likely to be reflected in the services they render in classrooms. Salary studies, studies of the economic status of the teacher[1] and studies of the teaching load[2] show severely depressing influences at work to lower the energy and dampen the spirits of teachers. In reviewing such studies it must be remembered that many teachers found it necessary during these years to carry the added burden of dependent relatives. Hopes for travel and summer study were dashed by the necessity of using savings for food and shelter. To add to the gloom hundreds of schools were closed; terms were shortened; and in not a few cases there were long-deferred payments of even the most meager of salaries.

The Field of Personnel Work

The field is almost as broad as it is important. There is the field of training. The education of teachers is not left to chance or private enterprise, but is made a function of government. For this, general policies must be formulated and expressed in statute or in administrative regulations; ways and means must be found and practical plans devised for carrying on this train-

---

[1] See: National Education Association, Research Division. "The Teacher's Economic Position." *Research Bulletin* 13: 165-267, September 1935

[2] See: National Education Association, Educational Research Service. Circulars Nos. 1, 6, 1931 and Nos. 5, 7, 1936. See also: Carr, W. G. "New Angle of Attack Needed in Class-Size Research." *Nation's Schools* 10: 27-30, November 1932

ing. Number, selection, and method of training in the education of teachers as well as the financial and housing plans for the service show a long and varied list of aspects for studies to attack. There is also the related task of getting into and of maintaining a suitable position in the service. Certification, appointment, assignment, salary, tenure, dismissal, retirement, leave of absence, and contracts suggest a group of policies and regulations to be designed and administered. These are related closely to problems of work load, competency, chances for advancement, and conditions of work. Also involved, are questions concerning freedom to teach, participation in policy making and administration, and freedom to enjoy the rights of a private citizen.

In this field, many interests are represented. Society, as a whole, is concerned with, and has much to do in determining, the social as well as the economic status, of the teacher's calling. The states have legal responsibility for envisioning, formulating, and directing the task of building and maintaining this group at a level high enough to produce the educational results desired. The local community, through its board of education, has special responsibilities and interests to be safeguarded. Parents, citizens, taxpayers, business and industry, and the children, not to mention innumerable special groups, suggest other channels through which depression influences may have affected this field. Finally, the teachers themselves, as citizens, as public servants, and as members of a profession, have important interests to protect. Although in the management of this service, authority and the direction of its flow are quite clearly fixed by law, control is not all legal at any time, and certainly not in times of distress. Influential pressures come often from social, economic, political and religious groups that have no legal authority but the right of free speech.

To picture possible depression effects upon the staff personnel it is necessary to see the complicated array of forces that play upon it. These forces are at work at all times, each through its own special channel. The teaching force is always, and properly, sensitive to those forces. By being so it is in the best sense an expression of the wishes of all the people. By this very fact, however, it is left open to attack from many angles and is likely to feel the influence of whatever disturbs the interests it represents.

Classification of Problems Provoked by the Depression

The problems that have been created in this field as a result of the depression could be classified in two important ways, either from the standpoint of a person or a group or from that of the particular interest involved. They may be problems for the state, the school board, the teacher, or for any other of the groups listed above. Again, problems affect some special interest. When the problems affect salary, pension, the standard of living, or terms of contract, the interest would be economic. When they affect the social status of the profession or of the service of teaching, the amount and quality of service provided, or the right to be a free citizen while a teacher, they would be broadly social. Freedom in teaching, training in service, tenure rights, and rights and properties within the service would involve professional rights and standards; and in dealing with rights and liabilities and the making of statutes, regulations and standards, the problems would be legal and administrative. For practical purposes it is well to keep in mind the two aspects of depression effects repeatedly alluded to above—what the depression did to the staff and what the schools or the people did about it.

Problems that Call for Research

Problems that concern society in a broad general way usually affect some particular group and some particular interest. Yet there have been some difficulties that reach beyond the scope of the legal, administrative, instructional; beyond the interests and responsibilities of teacher, superintendent, school board or legislature. The problems then become of consequence for the general well-being of society. It is the degree of importance rather than the locus of responsibility that puts a problem under this broader heading. A few such problems have appeared during this depression, among them:

Why have the people so widely demanded or permitted legislation establishing the loyalty oath for teachers?

Why have so many school systems closed their schools, seriously shortened their terms, or failed to meet their obligations to their creditors and to their teachers? The last part of this is a personnel problem.

Why have complaints about infringements of academic freedom become so numerous of late?

To what extent was unemployment of teachers a major depression problem?[3]

Why has there been such recent activity for and against teacher tenure?

Each of these problems has reached a stage where it is more than local. For no one of them is the depression a sole cause, but only a substantial stimulus. Several of these have reached the stage of being real issues among people outside the profession.

For example, a thorough study of the legislation to date on teachers' oaths is needed.[4] Beyond an analysis of legal provisions, this should include a study of debates and published addresses incident to the legislation and a review of newspaper treatments of the questions involved. A study should be made of the administrative machinery and processes by which these statutes are made effective in the schools. Although duplicating

---

[3] See: "Significant Facts Concerning California Schools," in *California Schools* 2: 27-32, January 1931

[4] See: National Education Association, Research Division. *Teachers' Oaths.* October 1936. Pp. 31. Mimeo. A collection of quotations from laws on this subject. Also see: Aiken, Conrad. "Where Civil Liberties Stand Today." *The New Republic* 83: 187, June 26, 1935 ′

such studies in part, there is needed a careful statement of the issues involved in the oath as a requirement and in the administrative practices incident to its enforcement. Such a statement of the issues should be accompanied by the published arguments on each side. Another study might determine what groups are actively supporting and what groups are opposing such legislation, and in each case, what interests are represented. It would be well to canvass the opinions of individuals on the question. What do teachers, school administrators, school boards, sociologists, lawyers, scientific men think should be done? Where these laws are being enforced a study should be made to determine whether the ills for which the oaths were offered as remedy have been cured. The question of who is to determine what constitutes loyalty to the constitution and allegiance to the government is a serious matter. When so much power by statute is placed in executive officers, it is a practical question as to whether one is not swearing allegiance to an individual rather than to a constitution. Thus research into the legal phases of the problem is needed. If this group of problems were brought together as phases of a broad research designed to provide a factual and reasonable basis for the issues involved, it would seem that some sound policy could be formulated.

A related problem of broad social importance is that of academic freedom in education. During the depression the number of alleged abuses of this principle has apparently mounted somewhat beyond earlier levels.[5] It seems reasonable that depression pressures might sharpen issues and that the working of this principle might more often stand in the way of needed administrative action. Taking account of certain types of legislation, of the frequent editing of textbooks in history and government, of the numbers of established instances of abuse, it is reasonable to offer the hypothesis that freedom in teaching

[5] See: Association of American Universities, *Bulletin* No. 2. 22: 101-106, February 1936. This gives statistics of cases before the committee.

is gradually being restricted.[6] If a fact, this is of far too great importance to our basic social philosophy to pass lightly.

What is this principle? Why is it important? How is it abused? Such queries have been widely and thoughtfully considered at least since the start of this century. Is it possible that the principle is inconsistent with the principle of efficiency in government, or in administration, and that it must be set aside in order that society may be managed? Is it possible that so often wide freedom in teaching is made a shield for those who seek to commit offenses graver still? Is it possible that to deny such freedom is the lesser of two evils? What specifically, are the alleged abuses committed under this protection? Looking from the other side, what are the alleged curbs to this freedom? There are the opposing claims on many cases where the principle is believed infringed.[7] A study of such cases with classification of specific infringements might be made. A law that communism cannot be taught as a fact is an infringement of freedom in teaching. If the law should merely provide against attempted indoctrination in the principles of communism, it would still be offensive theoretically because it left open the possibilities for indoctrination in other obnoxious social and political tenets. If it prevented all indoctrination it would seem to be fairer but, with present definitions of terms, is objectionable. Even with passion and fear left aside, it must be admitted that this question presents many difficulties—social, political, legal, administrative, educational. Research should be able to throw light upon these difficulties. Should there be developed a bill of rights for teachers? If real abuses of freedom of teaching are practiced, perhaps a second bill of rights should be designed to protect the

---

[6] See: Beale, Howard K. "Are American Teachers Free?" Report of the Commission on the Social Studies, American Historical Association, Part XII. New York: Charles Scribner's Sons. 1936. Pp. 855

[7] The Association of American University Professors, Committee on Academic Freedom, reports at intervals on this subject in its bulletins.

children; and then a third one to protect parents and our commonly accepted social theories.

Certainly studies of our statutes are needed to reveal wherein, if at all, this freedom is restricted by law. Corresponding studies might well be made of the rules and regulations of state and of local boards of education. Studies could be made of the possibility of abuse of freedom as well as of restriction of freedom. Such problems as communism, capitalism, fascism, democracy, even taxation on corporations, offer possibilities for abuse either way. Could all the major topics likely to be difficult and could all the student activities that offer opportunity for abuse be assembled and analyzed to find just what the difficulties are?[8]

Teacher tenure has been another storm center in this period. The interests and the issues involved are not new. The new element has been the severe financial and social strain under which tenure laws have had to operate. Inevitably, when people are plagued with troubles on every side they become sensitive to matters that otherwise would not offend. Fault finding on the part of children, parents, school boards, superintendents, principals and teachers would be expected to increase during a depression.[9] Does such irritability affect the question of tenure? This question could be studied and much light thrown upon it. For instance, did the number of dismissals for social or moral offenses, insubordination, inefficiency, increase during these years? Did the number of court cases, with tenure rights as the issue, increase?[10]

Concretely, it should be inquired whether or not the depression period has thrown light upon the desirability or feasibility

---

[8] See problem 2 in Chapter V.

[9] The psychologist would perhaps explain that the depression produced frustrations of many sorts in all these people and that when frustrated a board member is apt to look for a way to domineer over employees.

[10] See: National Education Association, Committee on Tenure. *Court Decisions on Teacher Tenure in 1935.* Washington, D.C.: the Association. 1936. Pp. 47

of permanent tenure by law. How have tenure laws operated in the different states?[11] From what abuses of the privilege of permanent tenure have schools suffered during this period? Have teachers with established tenure assumed attitudes and made demands over-reaching the reasonable authority of their positions? These and other phases of this problem should be studied.

The question of unemployment of teachers is but a phase of a large social and economic problem more adequately treated in other monographs of this series. It is a specially important problem for society, not in its general aspects, but in the fact that this group of workers is largely selected, educated, assigned to duty and supervised by public agencies. This governmental control is exercised because of the vital necessity of having the service continuous and thorough at all times. During the depression this service suffered severely. Its members will not soon forget the experience and their attitude toward their work is bound to have been colored by it. Not a few questions arise. If educational work is so technical that extended preparation is required for it; if it is so vital to society that it must be publicly controlled; then is it not incumbent upon government to see that its personnel is not demoralized by depressions? If this reasoning is sound, there is need to take stock fully of what happened to teachers during this period. What was the extent of unemployment? What was the extent of nonpayment of salaries? What was the extent of salary reductions? What happened to the standard of living? What happened to work load and work conditions? Had there been already a surplus of teachers? Are training institutions doing anything to adjust supply to demand? These questions and others, which individually belong under other categories, are a part of the larger question as to maintaining this special group of technical government workers.

---

[11] Numerous studies of tenure laws and their effects have been made. See especially: National Education Association, Research Division. "A Handbook on Teacher Tenure." *Research Bulletin* 14: 167-194, September 1936

Another group of problems centering about the economic status of the teacher needs to be studied. The salary trend in the depression has been revealed in part by competent studies.[12] There still are some partially explored areas, however, especially in the field of higher education, rural education, and private schools. More studies are needed of what given professional salaries will buy in the places where they are paid. This suggests a study of the cost of living for teaching along with a study of salaries. During the depression, school boards not infrequently gave the job of teaching to the lowest bidder. Such a practice is bad in every sense and more knowledge should be had about its extent. There should be a checkup on the status of funds from which teachers' pensions or retirement annuities are paid. How have these funds stood the depression? A study is needed of the use of interest-bearing warrants or other form of salary payment and of the penalties teachers suffered by having to accept discounts. Nonpayment or part payment of salaries was by no means confined to Chicago.

Was there increased activity of teachers in the direction of organized effort to gain advantages for members of the profession? Studies of the Teachers Federation movement, the development of teachers' cooperatives and credit associations are needed.

What happened to salary schedules during the depression? Were they dropped temporarily, suspended, or revised? Did the single-salary idea gain headway? What added economic burdens, such as caring for dependents, did teachers have to assume? What losses of summer study, travel, and other professional privileges or facilities did teachers sustain in this period?

There are problems having to do with the social composition, personal life, professional status, and activities of the teacher. What was the trend in attendance and in graduation for teacher-training institutions? How do these figures relate to the ratio

[12] See footnote 12 in Chapter II.

of supply to demand?[13] Has there been any shift in the social composition of the profession that differs from the previous trend? Are selections made from the same social, occupational, racial and intellectual groups as before? Did the ratio between the sexes show any change? What percentages of teachers have gone to summer schools as compared with the past? (There are data on this in many city school surveys.) What has happened to teacher participation in administration? There should be a study of statistics on the health of teachers through this period. For this there are ample comparative figures for other years. In such a study account would need to be taken of new administrative regulations affecting absence with or without pay. Have teachers generally taken more interest in politics during this period? Has there been a wide movement toward the left in social and political views among teachers or among school administrators? Have teachers been more often criticized for being outspoken in school and in public as to their social and political views? Not all of these questions will submit to exact treatment, but all will submit to some kind of study that will produce enlightenment.

A large group of administrative problems may be listed as properly here as in the later chapter on administration. There is need for studies of how salaries were reduced. What system did the board apply? Some salaries were reduced on a personal basis, dealing with cases individually. Some provided a straight percentage reduction; others a graduated percentage reduction. Still others exempted salaries in very low brackets, cut higher salaries first, then worked downward as further budget reductions required. There was an attempt to retain salary schedules as real features of contracts in some places, while in others such schedules were abandoned altogether. The question pro-

[13] Palmer, James B. "The Depression as an Incentive in Preparing Rural Teachers." *Nation's Schools* 10: 21-27, July 1932. Palmer shows how teachers are being forced into rural fields.

posed here is this: By what technique can a school system best carry out a systematic and equitable plan of salary reduction? Experience has been wide, prolonged, and varied and it ought to be brought together by an extensive study from which some general administrative as well as financing principles could be drawn. This would require study of the conditions surrounding the plan as well as the plan itself. It would have to take account of size of school system; the amount of saving that had to be effected; the reduction, if any, in numbers of teachers, carried out along with salary reductions; the schedule of salaries in effect; and of any special circumstances such as recency and amount of previous salary increases.

Another group of inquiries should center about the question of staff reorganization when retrenchment has been effected by reducing numbers. This is a problem in personnel management, but first it is a problem of general administration and comes to be one of curriculum, housing, methods, and educational aims. To solve the personnel problem these other problems must be solved first. Ultimately, though, the question of how to re-arrange work loads and how to dispense with services of least worth has to be met. A study of the results of plans followed in different school systems would be of value. Staff reduction was effected by dropping subjects, by alternating subjects on the program, by enlarging classes, by pruning subject matter and combining subjects. The supervisory force was cut simply by dropping much of the classroom visiting, omitting it where it seemed least necessary and by reducing curriculum revision work; the groups devoted to pupil personnel, public relations, research, visual education and other staff services were often either arbitrarily reduced or the services dropped altogether.

How has the university or the small college reduced its staff?— partly by not filling offices of those retired and by dismissing younger members. Precisely what does this do to the average staff? A good college staff, besides having the talent needed, should have as constant an intake and outgo as possible so it may not become unbalanced. A good staff has a wide age distribution.

Where the work load had to be increased, by what means was this effected? This would be a different problem in college, high school and elementary school; a different problem in different types of subjects perhaps. With this in mind, let the actual ways be listed with their various implications. Some schools lengthened the time each teacher spent in the classroom; some increased the size of class; some increased the number of periods of instruction; and some used other plans.

What has happened to the employment of married women as teachers and the dismissal of those who marry while in service? This became a more pressing question during the depression. A study of practice, of legislation, of school-board regulations affecting it, is needed.

Beyond these groups of problems there are others of more specialized interest, such as:

What has happened to the age distribution of the teachers of the country?

What changes were there, if any, in the mobility of the teaching staff?

Who were the unemployed teachers put back into the service by the Works Progress Administration education program?

What happened to the private teachers of music, dancing, physical culture and the like?

What changes were made in the state laws or state board regulations affecting certification?

An oversupply of teachers gave the opportunity to raise standards. Were they raised?

Did requirements to enter teacher training courses change?

Still another group of problems having to do with the organized professional activities of the teaching personnel is reserved for treatment in Chapter IX.

Methods, Technique and Sources

Such a list of problems, although centered about the single field of personnel service, represents a wide variety of contacts with the field of education. In many instances, with slight alteration, the problem suggested is approachable from other than the personnel viewpoint. Some are broadly social and economic; some bear closely upon teaching; some upon organization and management; some upon curriculum. The emphasis here is upon their connection with personnel service. These wide educational connections suggest the terms in which the problems must be studied. The values to be conserved are educational values, and only as other interests—political, social, economic—are associated with educational service are they of direct concern here. The educational check sought here on large classes, for instance, is not its bearing upon cost or upon teaching efficiency as such, but upon these as measures of the success with which the personnel functions and is managed. The concern with large classes also has direct effects upon the personnel, such as increased fatigue of teachers. Thus, answers to personnel questions often must be in terms of teaching efficiency, cost, curriculum, or guidance service.

From the standpoint of research, several types of problems are proposed. Some are largely statistical or enumerative. Some, such as studies of statutes and regulations, or of opinions and attitudes deal with facts to be obtained by analysis. Some problems involve evaluation or measurement of effects of increased work load, or of effects of low salaries on standard of living. Others seek facts to be interpreted in light of their broad social, political, or economic significance.

Techniques for handling such problems are mainly simple, though in many cases because of the character of the data, more than ordinary discrimination will be needed in planning the study and in selecting and interpreting the evidence. For example, is the American teacher more a liberal or a conservative in politics as a result of the depression? Perhaps there are no predepression data from which to start. In that case questions would have to be devised about the depression and its effects that would reveal whether the teacher sees society, the state, the nation, capital, labor, the poor, the helpless, differently than before. In general, teachers are in modest economic circumstances and have never been otherwise. Their work puts them in touch with the suffering of the people when there is any. It seems reasonable to expect that the depression would tend to make the group more liberal in its social, political, and economic philosophy. To test this hypothesis, however, is not simple.

Akin to the testing techniques is the question blank required in a few of the problems. Care as to the distinction between fact and opinion and as to the form of the factual question must be exercised. Techniques for the study of laws, regulations, published opinion or argument are well enough understood. Intelligence, more than the particular procedure, counts in all analytical study.

The sources from which data may be obtained are the usual statistical sources: government documents; personnel files of city school systems or of individual institutions; statutes and regulations and journals; minutes of proceedings of governing boards; and information from the personnel itself.

Sample Researches

PROBLEM 1

What were the effects of the depression on average student load per teacher?

One of the objective indexes used by accrediting institutions in determining the quality of teaching is the size of the student load. It is for this reason that the effects of the depression on the average student load per teacher has a special significance.

It seems reasonably safe to posit the hypothesis that the average student load per teacher increased during the depression.

Questions which should be answered are: How much did it increase? How did it increase for different types of schools, different communities, and different courses of instruction? Did the increase in average student load per teacher result in class membership that exceeded the standards for good teaching set by accrediting institutions? Did the depression have a relatively permanent effect on the size of student loads? Many studies can be made for individual states and communities which can furnish answers to these questions. As in the other quantitative time series studies suggested, however, it is important that the secular trend in average student load be controlled in order that the depression and the recovery influences can be observed and more accurately estimated.

Data on total student enrollment and total instructional staff in the public schools are generally available in most communities. They can on the whole be compiled also for private and parochial institutions. It may be difficult to secure statistics of student enrollment and instructional staff for the various fields of instruction. Important differentials may exist in this field, however, and attempts should be made to measure them. Two things to watch for here are: (a) the introduction of survey courses which might raise the average number of students per teacher without lowering the quality of teaching and (b) the possible elimination of numerous very small "frill" classes. This could increase the average size of the classes even though the number of pupils in the other classes remained constant.

PROBLEM 2

Has the depression with its increased load of work for the staff altered the status of the teacher in the field of administration?

Much headway had been made in this matter before 1929. It is the opinion of some that the depression caused boards of education to assume much administrative control not previously exercised, thereby trying to hold their executive officers more specifically to account. Did the same type of restriction go on as between superintendent and principal and between principal and teacher? Before the depression the theory of school administration that had copied its concepts of control from the older standards of military discipline was fast giving ground in favor of a theory of control that relies upon intelligence and understanding and cooperation and leadership, rather than upon delegated authority alone. The new theory has not been well formulated as yet, though it is evolving slowly in actual practice.[14] The difference between the two theories is substantial. If the depression affected the development adversely, it is highly important to take note of it now. What changes do depressions make in democratic trends of school government? It is perhaps important that this problem be studied without reference to depression effects but it is equally important to study it from the latter view also. Such a study should start with the hypothesis that the depression affected adversely the trend toward teacher participation in school administration. Testing the validity of this hypothesis will involve careful examination of its converse. The facts required must reveal precisely what former participation was abolished. What is in its place? In what ways have these changes altered the administrative principles at stake?

The first step is a thorough review of the literature bearing upon this subject. The second step would be that of gathering data to show the changes made in the services being performed by teachers, supervisors, and administrators during this period, and the connection the changes had with the depression. For this the sources must be mainly the persons themselves. Board minutes and personnel records will rarely give all the facts. It is not merely a question of whether the lists of duties assigned

[14] See an attempted statement of the theory in Sears, Jesse B. "Analysis of School Administrative Controls." *School Administration and Supervision* 20: 401-30, September 1934

were changed, but also how they were changed. Suitable forms should be designed for data on the different types of service, providing for the full listing of duties in descriptive terms and for indicating the bearing of each upon policies and their execution in the schools. Duties listed by teachers would be checked against those actually assigned to them as understood by the officer making the assignment. This would provide some safety against error or against reporting attitudes rather than duties or assignments. By a similar technique the study might also deal with the attitudes and opinions of teachers and administrators upon the principles involved and upon a list of specific ways of making the principles effective in practice. After all, it is not the assignment or the making of an assignment alone that counts. The attitudes back of it color the actual performance.[15] With these two collections of data, it should be possible to see what the depression did to established practice; the concepts teachers and administrators have of the problem; and how they are reacting to current trends.

PROBLEM 3

What was the effect of the depression on teacher salaries and employment?

It is clear that the depression forced salaries downward and increased teacher unemployment. To what an extent, however, was the salary level depressed? To what an extent were teachers unemployed? Which teachers suffered the more drastic salary cuts: men or women; elementary, high or college; teachers of "frills" or regular studies? Which teachers suffered the greatest

---

[15] See: Sears, Jesse B. *The Tracy-Union High School Survey.* Tracy, California: Board of Education, 1935. Pp. 216. This is a study of this problem in a single high school where a liberal amount of teacher participation was found, but wherein the teachers complained bitterly of the lack of just this privilege. The technique used in this study illustrates the above suggestions. It consisted of an extensive checklist of administrative services with possibility of reaction on six different connections with each service.

unemployment? Answers to all of these questions are unfortunately difficult to obtain on a national scale and even on a state or local basis. However, data are available which should shed light on a number of these problems.

The effects of the depression on the average salaries paid to teachers can be studied for the various school systems on a state and national basis from the data published in the Biennial Survey of Education. Local sources of data must probably be tapped for differential and more detailed studies. The secular trend should, of course, be controlled in such studies and comparisons should be made with general and specific economic indexes. Researches should also be made of recovery effects on teaching salaries. Moreover, in salary investigations it would be highly desirable to obtain answers to the following types of questions. Were teacher salaries curtailed more quickly and more sharply than the general or other specific payrolls? Are teacher salaries restored as rapidly during recovery? Time series studies in control situations may greatly clarify these problems.

As in the case of other time series studies proposed the secular trend can be controlled in such investigations by comparing actual depression salary level with the salary level which might normally have been expected if the "normal trend" had continued. It would be well, however, to also report the decrease in salaries from the 1929 level.

For the United States as a whole a number of standard economic indexes can be employed for comparative purposes. Chief among these are the Bureau of Labor Statistics indexes of factory employment and payrolls and retail and wholesale prices; and the Federal Reserve index of industrial production. For local areas local payrolls may furnish a comparable index or the incidence of relief may prove to be a usable index.

Teachers did not escape unemployment during the depression. This is demonstrated by the Works Progress Administration statistics which do not include all the unemployed, but which indicate that more than 40,000 teachers were certified as eligible for Works Program employment in January 1936.[16]

Although direct statistics on unemployment are not available, the Biennial Survey of the United States Office of Education does furnish data on total teachers employed and local records contain more detailed information on the characteristics of teachers employed. Studies of the effects of the depression and the recovery periods on teacher employment, in which the secular trend in employment is controlled, should furnish some basis for estimating teacher unemployment. That is, a projection of the "normal trend" in employment, through the depression period could be compared with actual employment during the depression. The difference would be an estimate of teacher unemployment.

In studies of this type it will be necessary—particularly in studies of elementary schools—to check the trend of school age in the population, since the number of elementary school students is largely a function of the age composition of the population and the number of elementary school teachers is a function of the number of such students. Corrective factors could be computed for corrected expected employment, if necessary. Here again the data should be related to economic indexes of the type described above and efforts should be made to get at differential unemployment by field of instruction, type of school and type of community.

PROBLEM 4

Has the principle of academic freedom or freedom of teaching been more often or more seriously abused during the depression?

Various aspects of this problem have been examined above. Of late it has been in the foreground of discussion. Several ap-

---

[16] *Usual Occupations of Workers Eligible for Works Program Employment in January, 1936.* Washington, D.C.: Works Progress Administration. 1937

proaches are open to research. Where is the evidence? What are the restrictions themselves? What are the channels of restrictions? Who or what interests are promoting restrictions?

The avenues open to the exercise of limitation on academic freedom are few. General laws, administrative regulations, and government by persons direct are the channels of authority. These channels, together with the courts, are the only ones through which legal control can be effected. It is well known, however, that laws are often but crystallized public opinion. Therefore, public opinion, the channels for which are the press and forum, becomes another agency through which coercion can be exercised.

These avenues are not equally open to restricting agencies. Constitutional law is difficult to change and requires much time. Statutes are less difficult to enact or to repeal. Administrative codes are easily changed; they attract less attention when altered; and they can strike directly and in very specific ways. Because it is single and personal and has power to conclude matters without notice, personal control is most open to abuse. Through interpretation it often overreaches law until stopped by courts.

A separate study for each of these channels or means might properly be made to determine wherein freedom of teaching is safeguarded and wherein it is restricted. When is a law actually restrictive? We have laws that provide what subjects shall be taught; what textbooks may be used; and that require specific activities such as saluting the flag and observing holidays. Certainly the laws imply, if they do not specify, that democracy shall be taught. Does the law mean that the child is to be prejudiced for democracy or against some other social theory? Is there any law or any state or local board regulation that guarantees the teacher full freedom of teaching? Perhaps freedom is demanded without defining it or examining the implications of any proper definition of it in actual use.

Studies covering these channels should clarify the principle, not alone in the abstract, but in its actual application. They should show the points at which restrictions are in effect and make possible a collection and classification of these as sources of safety or of danger. Similarly, these studies should reveal wherein we have established safeguards for this principle. Administrative abuses are usually not made effective through written regulations but mainly by direct personal control through specific orders or penalties. The source here should be actual and alleged cases of abuse and of protection. Reports in the hands of Committee A of the American Association of University Professors are one source of data for this study. The question of who or what interests are back of those abuses calls for a study of pressure groups. Studies are available as guides in this field.[17]

PROBLEM 5

What happened to practices for the professional development of the staff?

Reference here is to provisions looking toward the development of the staff and covering compensation, morale, work-load, working conditions and equipment, freedom to travel and study, recognition of creative effort and good service, and privilege to have a part in shaping the purposes, policies, and programs of the schools. Included also would be salaries, salary schedules, provision for retirement,[18] provision for sabbatical leaves on pay or part pay, reasonable leave without loss of pay when ill, op-

---

[17] See: Waller, J. Flint. *Outside Demands and Pressures on the Public Schools.* New York: Bureau of Publications, Teachers College, Columbia University, 1932. Pp. 151

Also: Pierce, Bessie L. *Citizens' Public Opinion and the Teaching of History in the United States.* New York: Knopf, 1926. Pp. 380

[18] See: National Education Association, Committee on Retirement Allowances. *Retirement Systems in the Depression.* Washington, D.C.: the Association, 1934. Pp. 29

portunity to participate in administrative service, reasonable freedom under guidance to experiment in teaching, freedom to carry on some outside study while teaching, public recognition and salary recognition for outstanding service, helpful supervision by competent leaders, maintenance of an efficient professional library, maintenance of reasonable work-load, privilege of attending professional meetings and the like. These things constitute the positive means whereby a good staff is developed and maintained for a school or school system. When a retrenchment program takes away one of these it is cutting into the forces that make for a high-class personnel.

It would be valuable if a direct study could be made of the morale of the staff. It would seem possible to devise a test or a related technique to study morale directly. A test which would register attitudes toward things done to the teacher and her interests as a result of the retrenchment program would offer a hopeful approach. This, however, would be a parallel study to the one here proposed and would supplement but not replace it. As a technique for attacking this problem it is suggested that a check-list be made of the above and other items, each item representing a supporting force in the total mechanism by which the school hopes to produce a high-class staff, and provision be made for registering whether such an item was in force and whether it was strengthened or weakened.

Chapter VII

Organization and Administration

THE list of problems for consideration here is intended primarily to cover what is commonly implied by the term legislation or policy making, organization and administration of both external and internal matters affecting schools (with the exceptions noted), and classroom management.[1]

Where the major purposes, plans, or processes of education were altered by force of the depression and where the nature of the program of education either as such or as a government function, or the nature of the government itself, was altered seriously, there have been created problems for the schools. The range extends from those involving broad social, legal, political, and economic considerations at one extreme to the details of internal management for a school or a classroom at the other.

Nature and Scope of This Field

There is a close relationship between this field and that of theory and philosophy of education as treated in Chapter III. The concern in that chapter was with the principles; here it is with the practical applications of principles. While some of the personnel problems of Chapter VI are appropriate to this section, they are equally well placed in that special group. The

---

[1] It is not meant to imply that the depression brought no problems in teaching methods. (See problem 2 of Chapter V). Wherever there has been a new project in teaching or a special stimulus given to the newer philosophy of education, there was a method problem. In most such cases, however, there was little that was entirely new, and there was not and does not continue to be the urgency for a solution that is called for by the greater social, economic, policy-forming, and managerial problems which now exist.

problems pertaining to finance and business administration, though properly within this area, are treated separately in Chapter VIII because of their extent and importance.

The scope of this chapter is broad, also, in the sense that it is concerned with the structural and managerial aspects of the entire institution of education. The service concerned provides for, directs, and evaluates the program of the institution or system. Anything that happens to education, or to the proper concerns of education, at once becomes of consequence to the administrative authority. In this area the vital relationship of education to the social sciences becomes apparent in a practical, as well as in a theoretical sense. That education is the division of our government which works constructively and at long range in solving fundamental social, political, and economic problems is now commonly accepted in theory and is becoming more and more obvious in practice. The very direct and specific application of education in the solution of social problems during this depression has been striking. It is one thing, however, to use education as a tool to accomplish some narrow specific result, and a different thing to use it as an independent and fundamental expression of society, as independent in its province as government itself. This relation of education to government is important. It may be disturbed easily when either government or education is disturbed. When someone shouts that our school books are praising another government to the disparagement of our own, legislatures are prone to act to suppress the alleged damage. When the schools want some corresponding change, as a better system of financial support, they must work by very long distance methods—by teaching facts—that require a generation to bring results.

This comment on the educational-governmental relationship will suggest like relationships of education with other branches of social science and is meant to call attention to an important and an easily disturbed area in the total social science field.

This depression has produced problems that involve these relationships quite fundamentally. For instance, because of the urgency of practical circumstances about us, we may face such a problem as that met by the CCC or by the wide plan of federal subsidizing of education without realizing that, by those acts of government, basic social, political, economic, and educational principles are being thrown into or out of gear.

The group of problems in this chapter is concerned with the efforts of government to meet the difficulties created by the depression. Both problem and solution become important objects for study if we wish to know the net effects. The range of investigation embraces the federal, state, and local branches of the government and involves some of these in new and strange connections.

Classes of Problems

Problems in this area can be listed in large numbers and may be classified in various ways. Here, perhaps more than in other chapters, it may be of advantage to discuss problems and their solutions separately. What happened to education or to schools for the most part has been antecedent to what the people, the government, and the schools did about it—much as illness is antecedent to diagnosis and treatment. Seldom can we claim to have foreseen and forestalled major problems. As depression phenomena, the difficulty and the cure are closely interlocked and are equally important. For study, they may well be examined separately.

What happened to education came as a result of direct economic pressure, because of shifts or developments in public sentiment, or because of social, political, and economic developments that affected the relation of educational activities to activities in other fields. Again, depression effects were registered upon education at different points and in different ways. Curriculum values may have been thrown out of balance, or new curriculum needs may have been created by social change; curtailment of revenues may have enforced retrenchment that fell upon schools in widely different ways according to public sentiment and available educational leadership.

This characterization and classification is offered mainly as a basis for approaching this field—as a set of major viewpoints from which to examine the problem proposed or from which to look further for problems not mentioned. Some of the problems are broad and general in scope (being social or political as well as educational); some have to do with matters mainly national; while others are essentially state or local in their bearing.

General Problems

Among the problems of broad general significance in the development of educational policies, either national or local, is that of a disturbed attitude of the people toward education. Aside from the people whose attitude was one of indifference, there were those who seem to have turned away from education and those who turned toward it. These two groups have viewed it with either unusual hope or unusual misgiving and their attitudes have been clearly reflected in the press, both lay and educational, as well as in the nature of the retrenchment programs and government-aid projects in the schools. In the face of this evidence of uncertainty it is wise to try to discover, if possible, the nature of this disturbed sentiment. What has unsettled the faith of the people in education or what has given them new hope in it?

Perhaps there has been no more and no less disturbance in educational than in social, ethical, religious, political, and economic beliefs and institutions. Time alone might effect needed adjustments. On the other hand, such a period of unrest offers an important opportunity to effect changes looking to social and educational progress. Do not these feelings of confidence and of doubt suggest, at least, that some changes are needed to bring education into proper adjustment with social and educational needs? Can research reveal the nature of whatever change there has been in the common faith of the people in education together with the reasons for it? This question is of basic importance in educational policy making.

This problem may be attacked directly even though no exact measures could be made of the rise or fall of confidence. Such a study would call for a review of what has been written on the subject. The literature would be classified, and then from each group of references the statements that reflect any disturbance of the generally accepted beliefs as to the efficacy of education in our government and social life would be listed. Views of statesmen, scholars, ministers, educators, experts in business and finance, state and local school executives, and of other groups should be examined separately.

This suggests a second very broad question: Have the things that have happened to the schools actually provided cause for loss of confidence? Hundreds of private and public schools are said to have been closed. Many of the more modern studies have been dropped. Is there some reason for people concluding that fads and frills have been a burden and that education has really not met its obligations?

The study required would attempt to find out what people think the depression has done to education; that is, what they think of closed schools, shortened terms, crowded classrooms, narrowed curricula, abbreviated courses, reduced health service, and obsolete and inadequate buildings and equipment. Have people realized fully what has been done to the character and quality of schools? Have they a vague and possibly mistaken doubt about the value of education and of schools?

There is a third matter that bears broadly upon general educational policy. In the recent public criticism of the schools pressure groups and the press have been active. This may or may not be wholesome in its effects. Education must never presume to be above criticism. Taking account of the deep conviction of the people long held as to the importance of education, however, such a flood of criticism should not be passed lightly. Who are the critics? What groups are represented and what interests are back of each group? Let their claims be listed and examined. Further note of these problems will be taken further on.

Efforts to solve depression difficulties suggest several other problems of sufficient breadth to warrant mention here. Has the depression resulted in a more severe self-examination on the part of the schools? Are colleges re-examining the major ends they have been trying to serve? Are the public and private elementary and secondary school teachers re-examining the objectives of their courses? One cannot review such works as the study of Recent Social Trends, the report of the National Advisory Committee, the National Surveys of Teacher Training, School Finance, Secondary Education, and the White House Conference on Child Welfare without raising this question. Has the depression given added impetus to the older movement of self-evaluation that really began in the school-survey movement at the beginning of this century?

Looking back at this period, could there be formulated a general policy by which the people in another period of like distress might proceed with the development of a constructive program of action for education? If, for the Federal Government and for each state, a list were compiled of the things done showing the period covered, the purpose of it, where it was in effect, the service it provided, the cost or saving it effected, the control, and the numbers affected, with an explanation of what was accomplished toward solving the problem in question, the raw materials would be had through which might be seen the plan by which this depression has been met. From this it should be possible to build up guiding principles and possibly the blueprint of machinery for facing a like future situation.

Incident to such a major piece of work, concerned mainly with facts, a careful study ought to be made of the judgments of those who have participated in handling both retrenchment and recovery activities through this period. Large numbers of these men and women are apt to be retired before such a program is again needed, or at least their memories will have dimmed. The registration of these judgments would be valuable. For instance, what is the judgment of university presidents, deans and professors on the net effects of the program of government aid to students? What is the judgment of congressmen and of members of school boards and superintendents of schools as to the wisdom of federal aid toward schoolhouse construction? What is the judgment of school executives as to the wisdom of each of the principal types of plans for salary reductions? Such studies of judgments need not replace studies of facts pertaining to these same things. These judgments are worth preserving as such; they are, in fact, a part of the explanation of the actions taken.

Another broad problem of public policy is the rôle education may properly play in handling the problem of unemployment. If there is to be a large number of unemployed, there must be policies for caring for them. If no public facilities are available for the use of the unemployed their spare time is not likely to be turned to the best account. A severe scheme of regimentation is not in line with democratic theory, but some constructive use of education would be. The development of guiding principles and a program of action are tasks greatly emphasized by the depression. This problem may be approached *deductively,* starting with the thesis that education is a basic element in our social and political theory and reasoning through to the ways in which education may function in connection with this particular problem. It may be approached *inductively* by collecting facts to reveal what unemployment means to the individual and to the community and state, and then showing wherein the solution of certain of the difficulties can be reached through education. Together the two approaches should reveal the policy needed.

Akin to this problem is that of making education a feature of all large work relief or public works programs. The CCC has shown that education can make a substantial contribution in this connection. The question of making this a regular feature of such projects is one in which educators, sociologists, and political scientists should be interested. Perhaps a suitable machinery for handling these projects as a continuous part of public service would need special attention in each state school system.

Related to the unemployment problem is the question of whether compulsory school attendance laws are in need of revision. Are there new problems that ought to be considered in the theory of compulsory attendance, and if so, how would this affect present laws on the subject?

It would be of some value to have a study made of when and how public opinion began to demand the defense and rescue of the schools. A study of the daily press, of secular journals, of educational journals, of religious publications, of special publications interested in the social well being of the people for an answer to this question would throw light upon a phase of recovery.

Problems Connected with Retrenchments

The depression greatly curtailed school expenditures. The results were closed schools, shortened terms, abbreviated programs, lessened facilities, and lowered morale. Was this unavoidable? Was it good management? Stock should now be taken of all that was done. What was the first act of retrenchment? Where in the country did retrenchments first begin? An answer to these questions for the country as a whole, and then as they apply in each of the various classes of schools—private and public, elementary, secondary and higher, each group being further classified as to size, type of program, and type of support—would be illuminating. Did public or did private schools start retrenchment first? How did small and large institutions of higher education compare; or small and large systems of public schools? Was the first reduction in cost similarly made in the schools of any one class? Upon what service did the first reduction fall? What has happened to the school facilities of minority peoples?[2]

In like fashion the period should be followed through to its close and the extent, the place, and the cycle of retrenchment should be traced. Some institutions and some school systems began to reduce expenditures much earlier than did others. If possible, it should be discovered, for each major division of the service, why some placed reductions in one way and some in another. When did salary reductions begin? When did curriculum cutting begin? When and to what extent were services such as the library, supervision, research, public relations, adult education, kindergarten, health education, visual education, special classes for the handicapped, first reduced? Any one of these items carefully traced for a single type of institution or system would be a research of value. Similarly, intensive studies of individual school systems should be made. If, by some suitable graphic method, a picture could be drawn of how, when, and to what extent retrenchments were effected in each major division of a school service or system, it would be possible to see the type of philosophy that really dominated American education. If, for any city school system or for many separate schools, the curriculum of 1929 were compared to the curriculum of 1934, a sharp contrast would be seen. To make this inventory there is need of complete and intensive studies of individual institutions, local systems, state systems, or procedures on a local, statewide or nationwide basis.

The data might be presented graphically in a time series, by plotting, on the same chart, a business index,[3] total school ex-

---

[2] See monograph in this series by Young, Donald, *Research Memorandum on Minority Peoples in the Depression,* and also monograph by Sanderson, Dwight, *Research Memorandum on Rural Life in the Depression.*

[3] Cf. suggestions in Problem No. 1. Chapter II.

penditures, salary payments, expenditures for housing, equipment, supplies, services provided, etc. Such a chart would show the secular trends and depression and recovery effects for as many items in the school budget as desired.[4] Absolute and proportional expenditures and per capita pupil expenditures could be shown.

There would then be the task of interpretation or evaluation. This might utilize a study, by checklist, of the judgments of board members, trustees, executives, instructors, and possibly of students or interested citizens. Probably the most important source would be the press. Other useful sources would be found in minutes of boards, faculties, and committees, and in publications, reports, and budgets.

Studies of single items or features of the retrenchment program over a wide area would call for a different type of research. A study of what happened to supervisory service in schools of cities of a given size might start with the hypothesis that retrenchment programs in those cities affected supervision adversely. First, a study of the budgets would reveal whether or not less money had been available and, if so, at what times. Other phases of the study could follow this temporal and financial study of each system. Pertinent here would be the numbers of supervisors employed each year (expressed also in terms of work load, as the number of teachers or of children per supervisor). Any changes that were made in the nature of this service or in the organization of the personnel engaged in it would be important also.

These inventory studies are not merely academic. There is certain to be wide variation as to how the various retrenchment programs were designed and put into effect. For these differences an explanation should be sought. In order to effect savings

---

[4] A sample study of this character has been made for selected districts in the state of New York by the Research Division of the New York State Teachers Association, Albany, New York.

for taxpayers, what was sacrificed in the program and in efficiency of service? Even though it may not be possible to express this sacrifice in quantitative terms, there would be had carefully developed factual bases for judgment.

Out of such studies workable procedures for effecting economies with the least possible loss to education could be compiled. Suppose a study of retrenchment in the plant-expansion program showed that the rate of increase in school housing facilities was slowed down. With a growing population to house, what happened? The lessened housing probably affected the service; whether the effect were adverse or resulted in more ingenious administration of the program, something of value would have been learned.

Such inquiries as the following would find place in this general inventory: Did children in states furnishing free textbooks fare better in the matter of using up-to-date textbooks than did children in other states? Like comparison between states with and without state printed or state adopted textbooks might be made. Did state institutions for advanced training raise the question of limiting attendance as an economy measure?[5] What happened to the schools conducted by business and industrial firms? What progress has been made in the cooperative work between schools and industrial firms that began in 1906? What became of private commercial schools?[6] What became of the YMCA schools? What happened to the school-consolidation movement? Was there any legislation that increased restrictions on budgets? When program curtailments are considered from the standpoint of the student, how did large and small high schools compare? What new trend was there, if any, in college-entrance require-

---

[5] See: "Finncial Retrenchment and Lower Grade Students." *Journal of Educational Research* 27: 430-34 February 1934

[6] See: United States Office of Education. "The Deepening Crisis in Education." Leaflet No. 44, 1933. Pp. 15. On page 4 is given an estimate that some 1,500 of these had closed.

ments during this period? What has been the trend in uses of school buildings for community purposes and what restrictions were made on use of school buildings by outside interests? What has happened to the holding power of the schools? What happened to class size? Some believe that through this period boards of education rather than administrators have been active in making decisions. Is this true? If so, does it reveal timidity or dullness on the part of our executives or loss of confidence in them by boards?

Problems Dealing with Efforts at Adjustment or Recovery

The difference between what happened to schools and what people or schools did about it, is partly a matter of viewpoint. At the same meeting, a school board may have reduced the personnel, set up a plan for providing additional adult instruction, and another plan for some particular depression adjustment. Caring for some matter connected with the existing program is different from caring for an entirely new problem. The schools themselves have not taken on many new problems outside of broadening and extending the scheme of adult education, and providing further education for graduates. Mainly, they have tried to hold fast to the initial program with as little pruning as possible. Many new things have been undertaken, however, by other branches of the government. Most of these mark entirely new projects in education and have been actual expansions in free schooling. Some of these projects are largely educational; others only partially so. There are many questions that center about these new projects and their management, as well as about constructive reorganization or redirection within the established schools.

In general, college enrollments decreased in 1931 to 1934 but this trend was more marked in some types of colleges than in others.[7] Tuition plays a far larger part in total income in some

---

[7] For summary statistics on college enrollments see footnote 2 in Chapter II.

colleges than it does in others.[8] Some of the smaller colleges were so seriously affected that major action was required. Actual mergers of several institutions were effected. The full extent and the implications of this movement should be studied.

When the depression first started, school officials tried to prevent budget reductions and to reassure the public that the schools would continue as usual. Later when public demand for tax reductions resulted in lower school budgets, the public again was assured that the school program would not suffer. As a public relations problem these announcements and explanations should be evaluated. Was the problem faced by boards and superintendents merely to stop fright and prevent undue destruction of educational service? Was it to inform in a true sense? Finally, what did this false reassurance accomplish? Did it lead people into the belief that a reduced school budget would not impair education? Did suspicion develop that the schools had been too elaborate and wasteful? Was the result an understanding that in reality the school program had been set back? Public relations programs should be laid out with regard for long distance as well as immediate effects.

This has been a major problem in public relations service and even though few accurate measures of results can be made, a thoroughly informing picture of it can be developed from a study of the publicity used. Intensive studies of individual school systems or wider studies would be illuminating to school and government officials and to the public. One is tempted by the hypothesis that school publicity failed to subdue fear, failed to thwart damaging reductions of programs, and actually built up a feeling that the schools had merely discarded useless fads and frills. A study of just what state and national school officials did to give intelligent direction to retrenchment programs would be useful. What did they propose as the wisest means of reducing costs?

---

[8] See Chapter VIII, Problem 2

As the schools were plunged deeper and deeper into the depression some constructive changes must have been made through legislation. Were any further educational requirements attached to child-labor laws? Were the compulsory attendance ages changed? Were additional provisions made for expanding junior college service? Was there any legislation affecting continuation schools? Were the administrative powers of state and national school officials expanded so that they might more effectively handle depression problems?

In order to meet the need gradually being felt for services not provided for in law, planning boards, citizens' councils, and other special groups were organized. Studies should be made of these new agencies wherever they contacted education.[9] The interpretation of the place of education in a national or state plan, as conceived by planning commissions, should be of value as an expression of the views of one group of intelligent laymen.[10] A large number of social and business organizations have educational committees. It would be of interest to know about the work of such committees during this period. Mainly, these are local and no doubt their part was played in local communities. The question is: Have they demonstrated ability to render important educational service in a depression? If so, they should be taken into account in a national plan designed to meet future emergencies.

During the depression, despite the wide use of newspapers, radio, and the cinema, as avenues for spreading information, there was confusion everywhere as to immediate procedure. How did the people react to this confusion? Did communities

---

[9] See: National Education Association, Educational Policies Commission. *Activities of State Planning Boards in Connection with Education.* March 1936. Mimeo.

[10] See: *Report of National Resources Board on State Planning.* Pp. 246, 265. Also see: reports of State Planning Commissions for Michigan, Oregon, Kansas, Illinois, Iowa, Pennsylvania, Arkansas, Ohio, and others.

organize information bureaus? Did they open public forums? Did they arrange for public bulletins? Did they use press, radio, theater, and school in new ways in order to bring the people together for constructive planning? Did people generally expect the Federal Government to care for everything? Did the old frontier method of local action and self-reliance disappear? Such questions have importance for education in a broad sense; for if people have become less self-reliant, if neighborhoods, as real social forces, are losing their vitality, the schools should take note of this in their programs.

Other questions that arise in the classroom may be asked at this point. Has the depression produced new problems that have to do with the emotional life of the child? Anxiety in the home and lowered vitality due to insufficient food would create mental-hygiene problems.[11] What new teaching devices and methods have been developed in handling the large classes that have been necessary during this period?

Sample Researches

PROBLEM 1

Have the people displayed less faith in and less enthusiasm for education than formerly?

Certain indications lead to this question. Retrenchment was loudly demanded of the schools relatively early in the depression. Appeals came early to stop school-building programs. There was vigorous criticism of the schools and school boards. The cause of education was not seriously championed by the press until well toward the beginning of recovery. The Federal Government proposed millions for special educational activities but revealed extreme reluctance to aid the schools directly. It

---

[11] See: Schumacker, H. C. "The Depression and Its Effects on the Mental Health of the Child." *Mental Hygiene*. April, 1934. p. 287. For a further discussion of this problem see monograph in this series by Stouffer, Samuel A., *Research Memorandum on the Family in the Depression*, Chapter IV.

may well be asked whether the people have lost faith in education or whether the enemies of free schools exercised exceptional leadership in building up opposition to education even among those who hitherto had relied most heavily upon it.

Many conditions, notably the inability of college and high-school graduates to get work, were responsible for the idea that education is no panacea for society's ills and is of doubtful value to the individuals receiving it. Regardless of the possible explanations, education has perhaps never in this country received more vigorous criticism. Were the American people of the past, as well as the present, wrong in the value placed upon education? Were these clamors against schools the voice of the people or the voice of carefully organized interests desiring to injure the cause of free schools?

Incident to these questions, research which throws light on public opinion on the following issues, should be encouraged:

1. Are free schools as essential to democracy as had been thought?

2. Are schools so out of touch with social realities that their product is relatively useless?

3. Are the people too little informed as to school objectives?

4. Are the enemies of tax-supported schools becoming stronger, more open, and more vigorous in their attacks?

5. Are the schools moving intelligently toward the task of offsetting criticisms, toward a public relations program that will maintain the confidence and good will of the people?

A major hypothesis might be: Because of this depression, education, and so the school, has lost much of the high value formerly attributed to it by the people. To test this hypothesis several studies suggest themselves:

1. A study of the editorial treatment education received in the leading journals and daily papers. At what time in the depression period did the subject first receive treatment? Was the treatment

favorable or unfavorable? Did it remain constant in attitude? Did it become more or less insistent? When did it end or change?

2. A study could be made by applying the technique used by the Institute of Public Opinion in the recent political campaign. Such a study of public opinion, if questions were properly formed, might bring before the public the predicament of their schools and serve as a preliminary to a public relations program. These opinions also would reveal the state of mind of the people on questions which, if the trend continues, will become issues in school legislation and in school-board decisions.

3. A study might attack directly the task of determining whether public education has definite enemies; who they are; their facilities and their methods for attacking education; their attitude on the question of free schools; and their connections with the people, politics, and pressure groups. This would overlap the first study suggested, but extend beyond it. Sources would include the organizations involved and their publications.

PROBLEM 2

When a retrenchment program for schools is required, in what temporal order should the items on that program come and what part of the reduction should each item bear?

The hypothesis here is: Worthwhile retrenchment policies can be formulated on the basis of a study of recent retrenchment programs and the judgments of those who made and administered them.[12]

A technique is needed for determining when retrenchment is desirable. To determine the economic situation is a problem in finance. To determine how to handle and when to yield to public demand is a problem in public relations.

Future retrenchment, if any, should benefit by retrenchments experienced in the recent depression. The major school budget

---

[12] For example see: Massachusetts State Department of Education. *Summary of Survey of Economies or Retrenchments in Education Adopted between January 1, 1932 and April 1, 1933.* Boston: the Department, 1933. Pp. 17. Mimeo. The answers to ten questions involving depression retrenchments sent to cities and towns of various sizes.

divisions might be set up, and under each division a large number of separate items (materials and services) that have to be purchased might be listed. On the right of these items there might be columns showing for each year, separately, beginning with 1928, the amount spent for the item. The more details listed, the more clearly the variety in practice would appear. When these forms were completed for the group of cities to be studied, all figures could be expressed as percentages of 1928 figures. Tables might be prepared showing the range in variations, and average or median variations. It would be interesting to discover the variations from city to city[13] and to find explanations for them.

A similar set of forms might be used to register judgments of school superintendents and business managers on the best plan to recommend to the people responsible for facing a like situation at some future time. These judgments would register an educational and an economic view of the problem in each city.

With such an analysis of past experience and judgments on how to handle the problem it should be possible to plan, in some form at least, sound guiding principles for formulating and administering a retrenchment program. Data for the financial part of this study would have to be compiled by competent accountants, preferably those in charge of business offices of the schools studied. The preparation of the checklists and forms would require some study of budgets and of the literature discussing depression economies.

---

[13] For what was done in one city see: Boston Public Schools. *Annual Report of the Superintendent, 1933.* "Depression and Recovery." Boston: School Committee. Pp. 6-15. (This gives a full statement of retrenchments made in supplies, maintenance, construction, etc.)

Chapter VIII

Problems in Finance, Business, and Properties

BECAUSE the depression was a disturbance of economic values and processes, its most direct effects upon the schools were through its influence upon income and properties and upon the source from which income was derived. Support of schools in this country is received chiefly from taxation, endowments, tuition, and donations. Earnings incident to the operation of properties might be an additional source, though as a rule such income is earmarked for specific services.[1]

Nature and Scope of This Field

The effect of the depression upon any one of these sources would vary widely from place to place. There are thousands of different taxing areas, large and small, rich and poor, some anxious to have good schools; others indifferent. Further, they have many different methods by which the taxes are raised. Some of these are far from equitable; others are reasonably fair. Resources from which taxes are drawn also vary widely from place to place. Some sources are constant and dependable; others are changeable and unreliable. Some communities are built around one single industry; others are built around many industries. Resources and population are growing in some and declining in others. Normally, the tax required for schools is great in some

---

[1] Income from dormitories, boarding houses, and the sale of stock or produce in some private schools may be sources of importance. Appreciations in values of securities held or of income properties would be a yield on endowments. Such appreciations are often offset by depreciations at other times.

and small in others. With these variations it is easy to see that a depression would affect such public revenues in widely different ways.

Much the same is true of trust funds. What they can be made to produce depends on the wisdom with which they are invested. These funds are held by hundreds of different school boards. These boards differ in their understanding of investments, as to their opportunities and facilities, and in the pressure put upon them to make the funds productive. Usually these funds are received in the form of securities or properties, good and bad. Obviously, such investments are not equally resistant to depressions. Tuitions vary with attendance as well as in amount charged; so if a depression affects attendance, tuition is in turn affected. Donations are not equally sensitive everywhere. Some schools have many friends and others few. Some schools are fortunate in having very wealthy friends; others are not so fortunate.

Besides varying in respect to each of these sources, the schools vary widely as to the relative importance of each of the sources used. The strictly private-enterprise schools have no support from public funds and seldom a genuine endowment. Independent institutions and church schools depend upon gifts and bequests, permanent endowments, and tuition. Only in special cases and in restricted ways do they receive funds from public treasuries. Public schools depend almost solely upon taxes. When one considers the bases of support as the point of attack in a depression, it is clear that schools are not equally safe at all points.

Any disturbance of the sources of revenue must have immediate consequences for the school. With severely reduced expenditures, curtailment of services is inevitable. Facilities for work are likely to be less well maintained and operated, and salaries and wages will be reduced. Finally, with pressure still increasing, reductions have to be made in the services supported.

All along this line decisions must be made as to what to do and how to do it. Some of these problems are financial; others broadly economic. Some are essentially business problems; others are educational. Estimating income and judging investments are financial; developing a plan for reducing maintenance costs is largely a business problem. Determining a plan for reducing instructional supplies, the salary budget, or services is an educational problem. Yet all these have to do with finance.

For treatment in this monograph, these problems have been distributed among the chapters that fit the special interest or point of emphasis of the problem. The concern in this chapter is with income in all its aspects, with property and its maintenance, and with the business service. Plans for economizing or for expansion that seriously affect the educational program are treated under administration or staff personnel.

What the depression did to sources of income and to the methods used for its development and control is of first importance. But with a study of such effects must go a study of what was done to care for the difficulties as they appeared. It is important to know how financial resources bore the depression and how the financial machinery operated. It is equally important to study the plans and devices by which new educational needs were faced or by which support was found where original resources failed.

Problems of Broad Social Policy

There are financial problems that concern the statesman as well as the educator. Both regard education as an essential public service. Obviously support must come from the public. How much of the social income should be invested in this service? The national income varies from year to year. Before the depression as high as two and one-half per cent of this income was expended for schools.[2] What has been the trend of school

---

[2] See: National Education Association, Research Division. "Estimating State School Efficiency." *Research Bulletin* 10: 84-85, May 1932

expenditures through this period? The value of the dollar is involved if the amount is thought of in terms of what it will purchase. There would be equally good reason for considering what the trend in expenditures has been for other public services such as road building, general government, or charities and reforms.

As a matter of public policy, spending for schools is much like spending for food, shelter, and clothing; the range can be from necessity to luxury. The amount required to maintain a level of culture sufficient to support democratic institutions would be regarded as necessitous. Any amount beyond this would provide a margin of safety. There is need for a better understanding of what this necessity program is and what it costs.[3] Although such a program is not constant in amount or cost, perhaps there is a fundamental relationship of the program to life. Perhaps there is also a fundamental relationship between its cost and the national income, or of its cost as one item in the necessity budget. With such a basic cost defined, there should be a picture of what is required to guarantee present standards of culture. What needs should be added to raise this standard? All this is now vague, but that is why it should be studied.

With such a concept of education as a public service, it is apparent that the necessity program ought to be regarded as such and lowered only when there is a willingness to lessen the national safety. Beyond this program it should be considered proper to lower educational costs only when depressions seriously reduce the net national income.

It seems obvious that in the coming years, national income is going to become a more active basis for considering matters of broad general policy. It is inevitable that more of the national income must go for public spending, and it ought to be spent in terms of careful planning.

---

[3] See: Morrison, Henry C. *School Revenue*. Chicago: Chicago University Press, 1930. Chapter 5. Also see: Carr, William G. *School Finance*. Stanford University Press, 1933. Chapter 2.

The question of public spending raises another equally broad question. Many systems of support for schools, public and private alike, failed during this depression. It has been suggested that such an important service as education should be financed in a way that would guarantee its continuous safety. There are two pertinent questions: (1) In a crisis can people be trusted to save schools by prompt and vigorous action regardless of sacrifice involved? (2) If the people are not dependable at such a time, can this guarantee be established by some plan of reserve or permanent endowment?

To answer the first question necessitates a study of the place education was given in this depression.[4] Did the people rally to its support in order to prevent serious loss of school opportunity? At first the schools were attacked vigorously, as far too expensive, or even wasteful. Comparisons may be difficult, but they might show roughly the sentiment of the people and indicate something as to the safety of the schools in times of stress.

No doubt there has been wide variety in practice. Salary reductions in some schools and colleges were made early; in others very late. Some reductions were large; others negligible. The same is no doubt true of salaries of employees in government service. Facts gathered over wide, representative areas would show what actually happened. History proves it reasonably certain that the people mean to stand by public education. Facts are needed now to show to what extent they have stood by in these trying years.

The second question is an old one but is raised in a new connection here. The idea of endowments was an ancient one before the days of public schools. In this country the idea of using public lands as endowment for public schools was widely applied. The history of those endowments has not been reassuring. That endowments can be maintained, if the people will it, seems reasonably certain. That such funds are difficult to safeguard

---

[4] See Problem 1 in Chapter VII

is equally certain. There are many arguments for and against the use of endowments. These arguments involve actual cost, equitable distribution of cost, difficulties of management, and safety. It would be well to study the success of many private endowments and at least some of the public ones, as compared with the severe set-back that education received in this crisis. Where natural resources (e.g., minerals and oil) are being permanently depleted, is there justice in the claim that at least part of such resources should be capitalized and use made of their income only? Why, it is sometimes asked, should one or two generations be allowed to exploit the full mineral resources of a state? Once extracted, the natural wealth is depleted irrevocably. It may be argued that by extracting and capitalizing the minerals a service has been done. Does history bear this out?[5] What other bases are there for creating such funds? Can an investment plan be devised that will guarantee an income of real value in such times? Moreover, if this principle is applied to the financing of public education, then what about applying it to other public services? Problems like these, of course, take us into the general field of finance, and to some extent may be outside the immediate field of the student of education proper. The results of such studies would be of deep concern to workers in education.

Research in School Support and Properties

Extensive research is needed to determine the relative merits of each of the main sources of support mentioned at the beginning of this chapter, as judged by their behavior in this depression. In some states local support is the chief basis of revenue; in others state support is the main source. Between these extremes are various degrees in the application of the principle of pooling the burden. In which of these states did support break

---

[5] For a consideration of this viewpoint see: Sears, Jesse B. "Financing Public Education." *Utah Educational Review* '18: 332-35, April 1925

down most quickly or to the greatest degree? In which did the opposite happen? Other things being equal, the state with the largest degree of district support and with the smallest percentage of consolidated districts should have been the one in which relatively the sharpest and the most severe retrenchments occurred.

State school revenues are obtained by several methods. In some states taxes are specifically earmarked for schools; in others no specified school tax exists, the funds being provided by legislative appropriation. What are the relative merits of these methods? Taxes on general properties, gross and net income, various sales, luxuries and severance are in use for school purposes. How effective has each of these proved to be? Actual productivity of revenue would be the main test.

There is also the question of what happened to the base of the tax. What happened to property, sales, extraction of minerals and oils, or personal and corporate incomes? There should be thorough studies of all of these, year by year, through the period of depression and recovery. Did assessment rolls sink relatively lower in one district, or in one county or state, or on one kind of property, than another? Did variation in decline of assessed wealth show relationship to amount of tax delinquency?[6] Was there equal delinquency in all parts of a state or over the country as a whole? How did decline in assessed wealth compare with tax rates and with decline in school expenditures? What was the effect of changes in property values, corporate earnings, amounts of sales, and assessment ratios on the problem of equalized cost for schools? Were these various types of support equal or unequal in their effect on equalization?

During the depression, opposition to taxation seemed to stimulate legislation looking toward the development of tax- and debt-limitation laws. At least a dozen states have enacted such

---

[6] See: Bird, Frederick L. "The Four-Year Trend in Tax Delinquency." *National Municipal Review* 23: 111, February 1934

laws recently.[7] It is often through such laws that the opponents of all forms of public spending work. The bearing of these prohibitions upon proper support for schools is important and a study of such recent enactments would be useful. One would expect such methods to be used more freely in a depression period. A review of court decisions, if there are any in this field, would be useful.

The abilities of states, counties, and districts to support their schools were much altered in many cases. Whether or not they will be restored to predepression levels is questionable. Ability in the form of economic resources varies widely. There were vast inequalities before and they still exist. This raises the question as to whether the task of equalizing burdens has been altered.

In the past quarter century, schools have used public credit in an increasing degree as a basis for capital expenditures. What effect has the depression had upon the debts outstanding and upon the credit of the districts in debt? To what extent have school bonds been defaulted in interest and principal? What part of this debt has been refunded? What is the history of sinking-fund support of school debts in this period? At what prices did school bonds sell at this time? To what extent was borrowing resorted to in order that current expenses might be paid? What was the extent to which tax-anticipation warrants, scrip, or other certificates of indebtedness were used? What losses did schools suffer through defunct banks? Other questions pertaining to depression effects upon public-school support will occur to students of school finance. The preceding list is varied enough to indicate that something, which could not have been learned except for the depression, may be learned about the

---

[7] *Property Tax Limitation Laws—the Evidence and Arguments for and against Them by Twenty-four Authorities.* Glenn Leet and Robert M. Page, editors. Chicago: Public Administration Service, 1936. (Contains bibliography.) The Research Division of the National Education Association has compiled some information on this subject showing that more than a dozen states have enacted tax-limiting laws recently.

strength and vulnerability of the various forms of school support.

It is clear that schools must be concerned with the ability of the people to pay taxes, but there are two other angles from which plans of school support must be viewed: First, to what extent the people desire schools; and second, the equity and economy in the plan for maintaining them. If a system of support is to be designed in terms of ability to pay, desire for schools, and economy and equity in burden, there is need to learn how to measure and to deal with these items.

In a few states the plan of support is embodied in the state constitution. In some states it is provided for in statutes; in others it is decided annually or biennially by legislation. A study might be made to show, state by state, how easily the school revenue responds to decline in desire for schools or to increase in taxes. Research should seek the relative sensitivity to changes such as these. A district system dependent upon a local tax determined each year might more likely yield to pressure than a state system, where a plan is fixed by state constitution.

Once provided, the method of *applying* school moneys arises. The apportionment of school funds rests upon widely different bases in various states. In some cases the intent is to equalize cost burden throughout the state; in others, equalization is effected little, if at all. Some states have special funds with plans for equalization. In any state, where some schools were closed while others were operating, it is likely, either that the plan of support is a poor one, or that the plan of apportionment has failed to equalize costs.

It is not the assumption here that uniformity is needed in plans for school support. Any plan should evolve in a natural way as an expression of the cultural interests it represents. There are certain basic facts and principles, however, in terms of which all plans must be judged. Schools must be continuously available for all children. The cost should rest equally upon the total economic resources, whatever they may be, without reference to who owns or operates them. The test of a plan is whether it accomplishes these two things. In many cases they were not accomplished during the depression. The research here proposed is a means of finding out what was wrong. Was the weakness in the plan itself, in the legal protection given to it, or in its administration? Was it in the amount of support the plan received, in the resources from which the funds were drawn, or in the inequity with which costs were laid upon the people? The systems that provided the best results should be studied for the basic principles they embodied.

There should be a thorough study of how endowments have withstood this depression.[8] Data on the permanent funds of public school systems and state universities offer a good field for study. The endowments of independent institutions should be studied also, but for this, small and large institutions should be grouped separately. Perhaps old and young enterprises might also be separated. The problem concerns the endowment, principal and earnings, through this period. Trustees of these funds probably have found wide differences in their investments, both as to safety and productivity through this period. Investment is a field of its own and it is not proposed here for research students of school finance. What is wanted is a knowledge about endowment control and management. How are endowments handled? Are there legal restrictions? Who makes the investment policies? Has good financial advice been widely employed? What is the control of actual investments?

Many institutions publish financial statements containing data for studies of endowment earnings. Did some institutions suffer greater losses of principal or of income than others? What varia-

---

[8] See: Arnett, Trevor. "Observations on the Financial Condition of Colleges and Universities in the United States." *Occasional Papers, No. 9.* 49 West 49th Street, New York: General Education Board 1937. Arnett gives special reference to endowment incomes.

tion was there in legal safeguards, administrative policies, and investment management between those institutions that rode the storm safely and those that suffered heavy loss? How did public-school endowments survive or produce income as compared to those of independent or church-controlled institutions?

Where endowment is a substantial basis of support, and where that endowment is invested in fixed-income type of securities, there is no chance for dollar income to expand or contract with rise and fall in dollar value. For such sources of support a period of depression may prove very serious when the point is reached where fall in prices ends and inflation begins. It is serious earlier too, because with decline in interest, bonds are likely to be called or refunded with much lower interest. This suggests direct study of what actually happened to endowments along these lines and a study of laws governing the management of trust funds. Were there laws that really saved endowments? In saving them did they practically destroy the institutions they were supposed to support?

Where mortgages were held the danger was of a different type. Either payment of interest or refunding is often impossible, and mortgagors find themselves in possession of real estate on which cost for taxes, upkeep, and operation becomes a burden. A study of endowment experience with this type of investment would be useful.

Gifts and bequests continued to provide new income, for higher education in particular, even through this period.[9] Such data have been assembled from year to year over a long period and may be reviewed with little difficulty. Educational gifts as compared with gifts for charities and other purposes suggest one point of interest. How income from this source has varied from that of predepression years, suggests another.

Income from tuition and fees has been so related to enrollment

[9] See: "Gifts and Bequests to Universities and Colleges." *School and Society* 34: 8, July 4, 1931

that a study of one involves the other.[10] The need is for an analysis of figures for institutions, grouped by size and by type of program. Small, medium, and large colleges of arts, both as separate institutions and as major units in universities; public and independent universities each grouped by size; professional schools such as those of law, medicine, divinity, teacher education, engineering, and mining, suggest types of groupings. How productive was tuition in comparison with its previous record and in comparison with other major sources of support?

In this field there is one problem of more than institutional scope which may be worthy of study. What was the trend of receipts from each of the major fields of athletics? This is perhaps more important as a phase of a broad study of what happened to the athletics program during this period.

In connection with income from tuition, there is the question of tuition loans. Attendance is an index to tuition but many institutions lent this money back to students in large amounts. It would be of value to know what amounts were lent and how productive these loans proved to be.

Doubtless institutions that operate dormitories, farms, or dairies, have need of analysis of income and costs of these projects but there is not an urgent general need for such studies.

There should be a study to determine what legislation, if any, has been enacted that relates in any special way to tuition problems created by the depression. For a time there was a demand that tuition be charged in secondary schools. Where local school support proved inadequate there was in some cases legislation that moved toward a larger degree of state support. The use of borrowing to carry current operating costs is not new, but borrowing that was specially provoked by the depression ought to be studied. Was there any change in laws controlling the care and investment of trust funds?[11] Was there any develop-

---

[10] See: Articles in *School and Society,* op. cit., on analysis of college attendance.

[11] California passed legislation by which Stanford University was permitted to invest endowment funds in common stocks.

ment of the earlier movement to provide dormitories for students in state institutions?

Related to support is the question of properties. At the beginning of the depression many institutions and school systems were planning, entering upon, or in the midst of, building programs. The need for this expansion varied but in most cases it was urgent. In many instances funds were available and construction continued; in others, for lack of such funds, it was halted.

A number of questions occur: What is the present status of housing as compared with 1929? To answer this for the country as a whole, a number of investigations would be required. There is the question of the amount of housing needed and the question, also, of type and quality. A study of the extent to which double sessions or half-day sessions were used provide one useful index. In such a study, care should be taken not to confuse lack of housing with other reasons for double sessions. A study might be made of the amount of building done in counties or states, by years, using figures from 1925 to the current year.[12] If building costs were used then the dollar value would need to be kept constant through the period. Where data could be secured the need for expansion might be expressed in terms of numbers of students.

Housing is so related to the educational program that the life of a building is not solely dependent upon wear and tear, but

---

[12] See: National Education Association, Research Division. "The Nation's School Building Needs." *Research Bulletin* 13: 4-31, January 1935. Here may be found excellent statistical data showing trends and costs in school building since 1918. The second part of the bulletin gives needs of school buildings as measured by condemned buildings still in use, part time attendance because of inadequate housing facilities, temporary structures of various types used for school purposes, ages of buildings now in use, need for consolidation of small schools, and a state-by-state review of building needs in 16 states.

Also available are reports of federal activities in school-building construction, one of which is: Von Struve, A. W. "School Building Projects Under WPA." *School Executive* 56: 94-95, 110, November 1936 also upon obsolescence due to its becoming ill adapted for service. A study showing the ages of existing properties would reveal in many cases a substantial increase in average age. Figures for original cost with dates and some description could be used with a depreciation rate and a fairly trustworthy appraisal of the plant could be reached.[13] Unfortunately, many county and state records do not contain really dependable figures for such computations.

In studying depression effects on housing it would be very much to the point to consider whether or not there had been overbuilding for schools before the depression. The loss or waste from this in the business and industrial world has been apparent in prices of building bonds as well as in the amount of vacant property and in the amount sold for taxes. However, the load for industrial plants fell heavily, while that for schools continued to rise in the majority of cases.

Research in School Expenditures

Some of the public school income is allocated by law to specified services. Endowments are often (at present in lessening degree) similarly specified as to use. Otherwise, education faces the task of budgeting, thus presenting an opportunity to examine the results of decisions as to relative values in spending for school service.

Freedom in determining how funds may be used has been revealed in a new light during this depression period. There are many controls over school expenditures that limit the freedom of administrators to apply their income as they think circumstances warrant. Tenure, either as law or custom, limits action regarding personnel. On the whole, administrators have found themselves narrowly hedged in at many points. A study might

[13] See: Strayer, George D. and Haig, Robert Murray. *The Financing of Education in New York*. Vol. I. Finance Inquiry Commission, New York: Macmillan Co. 1924

be made of all these controls or limitations and careful appraisal be made of the worth of each in times of depression. Possibly the hypothesis that there had not been suitable limitations of administrative control of school funds should be included, having in mind the danger of too little, as well as too much, restriction.

Along the line of balanced public spending it must have occurred to many that the necessity was faced for serious retrenchment in education as well as in other public services, with no norms by which to judge what constitutes relative retrenchment for education as compared to retrenchment in other branches of the public service. Can such norms be developed? Can a rough formula be devised by which a community of a selected type may know, in terms of reductions in one public service, what reductions are reasonable for other services? Is cost per person employed (arranged in comparable classes) greater or less in schools or in other divisions of public service? Does operating cost run higher or lower for school buildings than for other types of public buildings? How does maintenance of school buildings compare in cost with that for other types of public buildings?

There is need for cost studies that reveal trends. Salaries, operation, maintenance, supplies, or library expenditures plotted on curves through the past fifteen years and expressed in terms of an index, would be illuminating. Does this depression experience argue for a salary scale that is adjustable at intervals in terms of the value of the dollar? Should it be adjustable in terms of the amount of delinquent tax?[14] Has the depression led to the adoption of any new standards affecting the size of school grounds, or size of classrooms or of special rooms?[15] Did

---

[14] Suggested by: Cooper, William John. *Economy in Education.* Stanford University: Stanford University Press, 1933

[15] For a suggested technique see: Appendix, *Berkeley School Properties Survey.* Berkeley: Board of Education, 1926

demand for economy result in legislation favoring consolidation of sparsely populated rural areas or a wider use of the school plant? One might expect new legislation affecting budget development and control. The laws and the practices affecting accounting and auditing for school finance might be reviewed.

The chapter on administration referred to the need for studies showing what happened to the many separate services such as research, public relations, supervision, guidance, adult education, and others. All have a financial side and it should be possible to say for the country as a whole, in terms of amounts expended, what happened to these services. It was claimed by some that schools were too expensive. It might be possible either to establish the sources of waste or to show that they did not exist. In many instances, although heavy reductions in budgets occurred, the statement was made that the reduction "would not injure the services of the schools." Such a statement, if true, reveals serious previous inefficiencies; if untrue, it reveals a type of public management that is not desirable.

Federal Emergency Financing

The history of federal contributions to education should be written, especially as a basis for determining what policies, if any, or at least what reasoning, has directed these contributions. If no new policies have been established, at least a host of precedents have been created.

Each separate federal project ought to be impartially reviewed and then some evaluation of the whole made from the educational viewpoint. In what ways were these projects dovetailed into present systems of finance for education? Were they devoted to relatively new educational services or offered as aid to existing projects? Did they contribute to equalization of education costs? Were they conditioned upon actions of other government units? How was each project administered: as an educational project or as a phase of some relief activity? How did each of these projects start? Who thought of it? Who planned it? Who urged its adoption? If the Public Works Administration aid had not been provided, what would have been the present status of school housing? If student relief had not been provided, what would have been the probable result? What dangers lie in such help? How would school debts stand had assistance from the Works Progress Administration not been given?

Sample Research Problems

PROBLEM 1

What forms of school support proved best able to withstand the effects of the depression?

This broad and complex problem would require many separate studies. What forms of taxation were best? The basis for judgment would be the accepted canons of taxation, not as arguments, but quantitatively, factually, as they operated. While not simple to apply, their use would guarantee a thorough examination of how each tax (within the law providing for its use) contributed during trying times. There is not only the problem of studying the particular behavior of one tax and the area covered by it, but also the problem of studying combinations of taxes. The basis for judging any one tax or any combination would have to be on whether it met the purposes in revenue production for which it was designed.

A study should compare constitutional provisions fixing amounts to be provided, with statutes fixing amounts, and with statutes permitting the legislature to decide the amount. Other forms of control should be examined and compared.

A study should be made comparing state school systems on the basis of how the amount to be raised is defined. The formulas defining the sums to be raised should be compared first; then the legal machinery by which the formulas are to operate.

There are needed also new studies of the results of these plans of support. How well did they function? Did the question of equality of burden appear in new forms or with marked changes in degree during the period? The study must measure the distribution of the cost-load, and with it, the ability to pay. Numerous equalization studies for predepression times could be used as a basis for comparison. Finally, there should be a careful checkup on apportionment schemes designed to effect some degree of equalization.

If this group of studies were carried out for selected states, any new light that the depression may have cast upon our theories and practices in school support should be obtained.[16]

PROBLEM 2

How well did each of the four main sources of income for institutions of higher learning withstand the depression?[17]

The relative importance of each of these four sources (taxation, tuition, endowments, and donations) varies greatly from college to college. It is hardly likely that all endowments would be identical in their ability to produce income or withstand loss of principal through the depression. Nor is it likely that the streams of current donations have been equally constant in their flow to all kinds of higher institutions of learning. Taxes have not been as easy to get in one place as in another, nor for all types of schools. Income from tuitions has not behaved relatively the same for all. The reasons for these variations should be studied. If endowments should prove to have been the most dependable source; then perhaps there might be a desire to build up endowments for publicly supported universities, colleges and junior colleges. If endowments proved weak, and gifts strong, perhaps a shift might be made in the forms of philanthropy for education.

---

[16] See: U. S. Department of the Interior, Office of Education. *Research Problems in School Finance.* Washington, D.C.: The American Council on Education. 1933. Pp. 164

[17] *Depression, Recovery and Higher Education. A Report of Committee Y of the American Association of University Professors.* McGraw-Hill Book Co. New York. 1937

If, for each separate institution, the income from each source were tabulated and plotted on a curve for the years 1920-37, using some predepression year as the basis, it would then be possible to study their similarity or difference.

A beginning hypothesis would be that, in an institution of higher learning, its size, age, scope of program, and the degree of independence from public or from church control would be factors affecting the dependability of sources of income.

Chapter IX

Problems in Professional and Scientific Activities

HOW have professional societies and scientific work in the field of education borne the effects of the depression? Developments in these fields have taken place mostly during the twentieth century. Professional societies were small and inactive at the beginning of this century. Hundreds of teachers belong to these organizations today where only dozens belonged then.[1] The professional and scientific literature in education has had a like development. In the education of teachers, in textbooks and teaching equipment there have been great developments. This movement has now been through a severe depression. What has happened to these professional and scientific activities?

The Field for Study

While the country must expect the teaching profession to look after the social and economic well-being of its own members, it should be able, with equal assurance, to look to it for leadership in the field of education. If the profession has pride in achievement and hope for its own future, it also is concerned to know how it has stood the test of this depression. Did the forces of education scatter or rally? A thorough social survey would probably show that, as a result of the depression, hundreds of organizations—social, business, and professional—were actually, if not formally, disbanded and that few new organiza-

---

[1] The National Education Association, with a present membership of nearly 200,000 had less than 8,000 members twenty years ago.

tions (government excepted) took form. Such a study most
likely would show, too, that subscription lists suffered a substantial decrease for all current publications combined and for
the majority of them separately. What part of this picture did
educational organizations, educational journalism, and scientific
work in education, form? In practical leadership, what has
education to show for this period of stress?

Professional Organizations

A study of the rise or decline in membership of all the educational organizations separately and combined ought to be made,
showing the trend through a long period. Such figures as these
would need to be explained. Rise or fall in cost of membership
would probably be reflected in the number of members. Paid
and other memberships should be treated separately What
membership does for the member would need to be checked.
Increase in the number of societies probably would affect the
number of members for a given society.

The value of complete statistical analysis of such facts in the
field of education seems obvious. That such a study should be
kept abreast of the time is equally obvious, and suggests the
present need in the profession for a general clearing house for
information of this character. To collect, analyze, and report
such data is now the responsibility of no one.

Aside from what happened to membership in each educational
organization, it should be known what these organizations did
about the depression. No one was closer to schools and colleges
than those who were teaching in them or directing their affairs.
At the outset, the depression was not taken seriously. Long after
actual retrenchment had begun there was public reassurance
that the school program was entirely safe. This provokes the
question: When in the depression did the profession begin to
warn the people that retrenchment *was* damaging, or likely to
damage, the schools? Did such organized efforts as those of the

Emergency Commission come early or late? A complete story of the activities of the educational organizations of the nation should be written, showing when each began its work; how it cooperated with other professional groups and with government agencies; and what it contributed.[2]

Relating to this direct and positive effort on the part of the professional organizations, the resolutions passed by the many separate units during this period should be studied. If the resolutions of the societies through this period could be analyzed and compared with those of the preceding half decade, it would provide a basis for judging the vision and the aggressiveness shown by professional leadership in a time of need.

Aside from resolutions, which often are little more than a ceremonial reference to work that is going on in committees or to serious deliberations, there is need for a review of the work done on depression problems by these organizations. A study of committee work touching depression problems, and of the papers and addresses on this subject would be of value. What were the problems as they saw them? What facts did they present? What attitude did they display? In such a study, it would be of interest to know whether educators saw the problems of education in isolation, or whether they saw them as phases or aspects of the broader social problems of the time and place.

Related to proceedings and committee reports is literature found in professional magazines. What did the editorials contribute through these years? On what subjects were the major articles written? In what ways and to what extent was the

---

[2] See: Norton, John K., chairman. "Work of the Joint Commission on the Emergency in Education for 1935." *Proceedings,* 1934. Washington, D.C. National Education Association, 1934. Pp. 30-37. This is a report of the work of the Commission to date, with plans for the future. Explains support that was given to emergency legislation, conferences held, and facts assembled about depression effects. It urges first, solid organization to help secure adequate legislation on the school finance problem; and second, the reshaping of the educational program.

depression treated through these publications? A study of the decline in subscriptions to professional journals would reveal the extent of reliability of professional journals as a medium through which pertinent information and opinion may be disseminated.

A slightly different study of the professional writings might show how different interests appear at different stages. At the outset, professional journals said little or nothing about the depression. This was true through 1930 and early 1931.[3] In the latter part of 1931 news notes reported retrenchments and general discussions started of the machine age, a new social order, how to economize without any harm, and so on. A little reflection on the apparent inability to cope with the situation arising, makes one tolerant of the apparent confusion exhibited by writers in the early part of the depression. Normally, it would be reasonable to assume that if this depression had been merely the culmination of forces long at work, if those forces represented a genuine shift in social life, then inevitably education must first reinterpret its aims and objectives and then reconstruct its curricula. In the serious thought and work of educators, does the literature of this period show that such movements are in reality taking place? If this hypothesis is sound, a real movement for restatement of educational objectives should be well under way during 1937.

Because salary control has been local, salary reductions would vary widely. Variety in plans of support constitute other basic reasons for such differences. How has the profession dealt with this problem? Did national and state organizations allow local groups to fight their own battles or was there an organized program for protecting the economic interests of teachers? In a broad sense, this is not a question of the selfish interest of teach-

---

[3] One of the earliest, if not the first, published statement recognizing the coming dangers was the 1930 *Report* of the Secretary of the National Education Association.

ers. The reasonable protection of the group is a proper part of public policy.

A study of what happened to the work done by clubs devoted to local discussion and to reading circles would be of value.

Educational workers are not well organized. Teacher turnover is very large, and many regard entrance into the work as only temporary. For this reason many teachers do not identify themselves with the profession. As a consequence, the profession carries a heavy fringe of half-interested members. The result is lack of a common purpose or enthusiasm to weld the group into social and professional unity. Lacking the self-consciousness that comes only with such unity, the profession lacks drive and influence. This condition was greatly aggravated by the depression. There is still the task of welding the school people into a profession in its highest sense. Teachers should unite to protect their own rights—tenure, salary, sick leave, and retirement allowance. They should work together for the cause of education, especially when that cause is endangered.

Can the profession find a means of quick contact among its members; of quick exchange of opinion and judgment? Although the profession has dozens of journals, volumes of proceedings, local house organs, meetings, and resolutions, the question is unanswered. What issues or problems of importance received the full force of educational opinion during this depression? There is probably substantial unity of opinion among teachers on most of the major educational problems. Can that opinion be formulated so the public can be made to feel it? Can that opinion, when expressed, have back of it the force of a solidly united group? This expression of opinion refers only to education, not to politics.

The public, as a rule, does not read educational journals, proceedings, or resolutions. It seldom knows or even hears about propositions that affect schools. Can a technique be developed for registering such propositions with the public in order to obtain their opinions? A sampling technique could be devised, such as that used by the Institute of Public Opinion and through it important questions such as the following could be brought before teachers and the public. Should music and art be restored to the curriculum? Should consolidation of small districts take place more generally throughout the country? Should federal support for schools be introduced? Should the unionization of teachers and their organizations be encouraged or repressed? In view of social and economic trends, should compulsory school attendance age be raised? Should the health work of the schools be reinstated? School people also would be forced to inform themselves upon the major problems of education. They would, through participation in forming such opinion, be drawn into closer unity with the public. The public might become more aware of the teaching group and of its judgment concerning what is needed to make schools more effective. The development of the technique and the preparation of a plan for its use is the problem for research.

Scientific Work in Education

What has been the scientific activity and output in education through this period? With the beginning of the testing movement in 1908 and the survey movement in 1910, forces were set in motion that shortly resulted in a research service set up in many local and state school systems, individual institutions, and professional organizations. The subsequent development of this educational research service has been notable.[4] Research has gained prominence as an aspect of the educational program for teachers and for those preparing for executive work in the field of education. The numbers taking higher degrees and the accompanying body of theses in education have grown apace.

[4] Chapman, Harold B. *Organized Research in Education.* Bureau of Educational Research Monographs, No. 7. Columbus, Ohio: Ohio State University, 1927. Pp. 211

Educational books, including textbooks, monographs, documents, and journals reflect this development. Without presuming that education has developed into a seasoned science, it is clear enough that there has been a movement of great promise.

Has this vigorous young movement been disturbed seriously or turned out of its course, or perhaps destroyed, by this depression? One of the surest ways to stop or discourage scientific work is to close the channels for its publication. Statistics on the publication of all books, as well as those on education, show a decided decline. Though complete figures from publishers and distributors are difficult to obtain, there are some figures available. The very significant purchase figures for libraries are available. Some study of the publication and distribution of books could be made worthwhile if it could be shown in a reasonably accurate way how the decline has affected the scientific output. For the magazine output the case would be clear. An analysis of articles possibly could be made that would show what has happened to the quality of material.[5]

A study could be made of such movements as that of the school survey. Similarly the testing and the curriculum-revision movements could be studied. Never is research so important for education as when swift social changes threaten to topple the very objectives of education, as well as many parts of its program. At this critical time their curtailment did involve the very activities offering the most reasonable hope of gaining some understanding of what was happening. What became of city school research departments, of state school research departments, and of like departments in universities and professional societies? Where is this machinery, and what has been the output from these sources?

Lists of published and unpublished studies from these sources should be analyzed. Some of these have been assembled by the

---

[5] See Waples, Douglas. *Research Memorandum on Social Aspects of Reading in the Depression,* in this series.

United States Office of Education. Were research organizations kept busy compiling unimportant statistics or were the problems of major importance studied? In the midst of such stress there must have been born at least a few bright ideas that research should bring to light as examples of leadership.

Related to this are activities of the great foundations long devoted to research. These research agencies finance individual students and research projects; provide fellowships and publish research results. What is the character of the work done by these foundations during this period? Since they command the best talent, an analysis of their work would provide the best evidence of vision in solving depression problems of an educational nature.

The United States Office of Education, on its own authority and by special assignment from the government, has expanded its research service to education. Its regular statistical reports are substantial contributions to educational research. Just how this Office has functioned in dealing with new, as well as with old problems is worthy of analysis.[6]

Each of the services so far alluded to is an independent one. Although there has been genuine effort at coordination, this depression has raised so many questions that one cannot review these agencies without the suggestion that a real coordinating machinery should be developed. Such a coordination of research services would reach beyond the meeting of emergencies; it would build eventually a statistical foundation that would provide prompt orientation of forces and materials available at any time. Information could be disseminated that would add greatly to the capacity of each of these agencies to serve and to their readiness for action whenever need should arise.

The field of education has accomplished much since the publication of its first committee report in 1912 on the subject of

---

[6] See: Goodykoontz, Bess. "The Office of Education in the Present Emergency." *Proceedings*, 1932. Washington, D.C.: National Education Association, 1932. Pp. 160-62

uniform records and reports. Attention has been called to the need for a system of basic reports covering the activities of professional groups and providing a basis for effective coordination. In thousands of school offices there are carefully gathered data that could be used in research. Probably this is equally true in many other branches of the government, and in other professional organizations. No one person knows all of these many sources, what they offer, or how access to them could be gained. There is little doubt that much could have been accomplished in meeting depression difficulties had we had a composite picture of these many sources. The profession could prepare a handbook explaining where the sources are, their contents, their form, how they are developed, how they are controlled, and conditions under which access to them would be possible.

Do regular official documents provide adequate factual data on depression effects in their respective fields? Various reports of the United States Office of Education illustrate, by cumulative tables and graphic presentations covering years before and through the depression, what is meant here. If all national, state, and local documents did this effectively, it would be possible to paint a picture of the depression results on education.

Chapter X

General Interpretation, Explanation, and Overview of the Field

IT WOULD be contrary to the purposes that directed its development if this monograph were viewed as a mere catalog of isolated problems. The desire was to aid in the eventual painting of a unified picture of a brief but dangerous period in the history of American education. This volume does not relate facts about the depression and what it did to education, but raises systematic questions in the field of needed facts. It is hoped that no small amount of thinking about education, research, and depressions, separately and together, may be provoked to the end that education may profit by the lessons of the 1930's and face more intelligently any similar disasters in the future.

Purpose of a Summarizing Chapter

This project was started with the assumption that education had been disturbed either as a whole or in part. This appears simple if the assumption is applied to existing schools or colleges, children or teachers, books or buildings. It is far from simple, however, when the objectives of education are considered. Who desires schools and why? Where is learning acquired? Thinking of education as a public service, are educational purposes and mechanism related to the purposes and mechanism of government? Government and education are both designed and operated in terms of some chosen theory of the state, society, and education.

In many cases a problem exists in much the same form in more than one division of a field. In such cases the way is left open to decide in what special division of the total field a choice would be made. For this the following plan of grouping is used:

History of education with comparative studies
Theory and philosophy of education
Student personnel
The curriculum or program of instruction
The staff personnel
Organization and administration
Financing the schools
Scientific and professional activities

A brief explanation of each division will serve to show that, together, they cover the field of inquiry, and how each may serve as a point of departure for a group of researches.

The Chapters Summarized

Any study of depression effects on education must be a study of cumulative influences, and might be called historical. Chapter II presents a group of problems, the immediate aim of which is to contribute to the field of educational history as a professional study as well as to help toward the solution of future problems. This depression is too recent to make adequate historical treatment possible. At least the experiences of the period can be recounted in terms of facts and it should be possible to identify and classify these facts. Time only can reveal their final worth. However, there is the experience of previous depressions, many facts of which are unassembled, unanalyzed, and unevaluated. Any common characteristics of depression effects upon education should be known. Certainly many of the sets of facts would show peculiar shifts during such times. It is known now that some of those shifts are dangerous. The history of what depressions have done to schools and to education and of what they did about it should have great practical value, therefore, to those who shape the policies either of state or school.

With the backward look educators will need also to look to right and left. What has happened to education in other countries? Education can be related to the other elements of the culture in different ways in different times and among different peoples. Once education was basically related to the church in most of the world. Today it is basically related to the state. History makes clear how education may be independent in one type of culture and subservient in another. In a democracy, education must be free and highly independent. It obviously cannot be free in the same sense in any other forms of government. In the former the school is part of the state; in any other the school would be merely an instrument.

The student of comparative education must know what he is comparing. How do education and schools fare in the various types of political systems when all alike are submerged in a common depression? It is quite possible that a study of how education has fared in Germany, Russia, Sweden, Italy, Spain, France, England, Australia, Canada, or in any of the world's smaller nations, would enable us to see our own problems more clearly.

Chapter III presents problems in educational theory and philosophy that are established upon biology, psychology, sociology, politics, and economics; upon experience in living; upon our wishes, needs, and aspirations. When action is necessary and absolute facts and laws for guidance are lacking, a theory or a philosophy is the only guide. There is no ultimate settlement available, either of what ought to be done in education, or of how it should be done. So there is the necessity to guess and reason in light of what facts are available and what values would be desirable.

It might seem that depressions could do little to theories or to the facts of science; yet, they have produced new facts. A child may have been a normal pupil until the mental strain of poverty in the depression necessitated treatment by a psychiatrist. The government as it has been known for generations, is a different government since it has been forced to assume new services.

It is the function of educational theory and philosophy to keep the purposes of education and the bases upon which procedures rest, related to this mass of changing, growing, disappearing body of fact and meanings. Clearly a theory and a philosophy cannot be made once and for all. They, too, are evolving. Education is built by the life of the times and, both in its nature and its control, is related to other elements and units in the civilization of its time. What shall be extracted as the essence of life at present to teach as the basis for the good life wished for the coming generations? How shall the institution through which such education is imparted be created, controlled, and managed?

Since the aims and purposes of the school can be established only in light of theory and philosophy; since the curriculum cannot be constructed and a plan of control and operation worked out without aims; there is as much concern to know what the depression did to the raw stuff of which philosophy and aims are made, as there is with any tangible feature of the school itself. Are educational goals in need of restatement? With the altered economic status of the school and the altered relationships of government to the people, is the system of control and support out of alignment with need?

Chapter IV presents problems dealing with the school population or student personnel. The whole school enterprise centers about those who are served. The program of education is their program. Educational concern is not with biology and psychology in the abstract but with the biology and psychology of the students. Not merely the sociology, economics and politics of the established social order alone, but also of the school and the children in the school count for the study of education. Regardless of what is done, in what direction research turns, the start and the return is to the student.

The depression may affect the child by altering his capacity, interests, opportunities, or needs for education. It may affect him by changing the school so that its offerings differ from what otherwise they would have been. Education is individual and personal; but each student is part of the school society. As a part of a social group he is to become a responsible unit in many groups of adult society. In either case the task of learning has been changed. Until he is known, there can be no knowledge of how to teach him. Until the entire group as a group is known there can be no hope of organizing our schools intelligently nor of achieving valid educational purposes.

Chapter V presents problems dealing with the curriculum or the program of instruction. "What shall we teach?" ask the schools. "What shall we learn?" ask the pupils. History shows that there have been many excellent, as well as many strange, answers in the past—answers that seemed based upon the assumption that the student's question was a bit of impertinence, and that the school's reply was best when it was answered in terms of the most venerable of school subjects. Importance here, rested in part on the nature of knowledge and skill as tools and in part on their value as information and discipline. Here and there something was studied that equipped the student for practical life, but until recent years, the selection of teaching material on the basis of present worth to the child or to society was not the dominant viewpoint. Emphasis was laid upon knowledge itself rather than upon its usefulness to the student. Mastery of any subject was assumed to guarantee possession of a special virtue. These virtues were more often general than special. By study of spelling one was expected to become a speller of all words; not merely of the words studied. Some studies were presumed to have such broad virtues as to fit one for work in almost any field.

Curriculum makers have always had a theory to justify their choice and arrangement of subjects. One theory starts with the child and his own present special interests and problems, and moves through the stages the child must travel in getting answers to those problems as they lead him step by step in building himself a world. The world he builds will be his own, but since it must lie within and interlock with the worlds that others have built or are building, he finds many new kinds of social problems. He will have to recognize that his will is but one among many. It is now believed that getting an education is living through these problems. In order to solve them, the learner must know, do, feel, remember, and imagine. He must create and destroy. He must give and take. He must lead and follow. He must make his own decisions and abide by the decisions of others.

The depression found the curriculum in process of change. Since the curriculum is in reality a program of living, physically, mentally, and emotionally, among the essential facts and forces of this world, and since this depression has disturbed much of the social substance, it is reasonable to ask: What did the depression do to the curriculum? What did the school do about it?

Chapter VI presents problems dealing with staff personnel. Viewed either as a feature of organization or as a functional service, the school staff is an important element in the school system. Its contacts are with every part of the field, to be sure, but most of the problems that have to do with these contacts can be approached with good effect as parts or aspects of the personnel field.

There are many ways in which depression influences may have impressed themselves upon staff personnel. If the depression should give rise to new educational needs, then new or added workers would be required. Training schools would face the task of designing suitable curricula. If schools were closed, or services curtailed, then unemployment would result; jobs would become uncertain; and staff morale would be affected. If salaries are reduced to save tax money, then unemployment, lowered morale, lowered standards of living, less summer-school training and travel, may ensue. Under such pressures old issues are apt to be intensified and new issues to arise. Rights of tenure, retirement age, status of married women as teachers, rights to participate in policy forming and administering, breaking or changing salary schedules, the question of academic freedom and similar matters are likely to be raised with new emphasis. Under such pressures a general shift seems likely in the concern of teachers, to an insistence upon their rights rather than upon professional growth or efficiency in service. With an altered meaning of education, what happened to the teacher's work program? With an altered income, what happened to professional interest and effort? Clearly, one of the most important concerns of a community during a depression should be to keep the school staff in good health and morale. Upon this depends morale in the homes and in the community.

Chapter VII presents problems dealing with organization and administration. The depression has put an exceptional strain upon every social institution and upon its management. It was generally recognized that the financial foundations of public education were giving way; that the organization was defective at many points; and that a crisis would be faced within a few years. The depression simply hastened this conclusion.

While all problems of organization and administration are firmly lashed to the problem of support, school finance is so vast in its scope that it seems better to treat it separately. Further, this depression has made an impress upon the school machine itself, and upon its management, that will need to be studied from other points of view than that of financial economy alone.

Administrators have been besieged by old and by new pressure groups quoting new needs. These new needs called for substantial alteration of courses and curricula and class organization. Necessity for retrenchment brought a flood of administrative problems as to where to begin and where to end. Urgent need for employment among teachers with corresponding demand for reduction of personnel illustrates the confusion faced.

What was really accomplished by the changes? Were the newest things saved or were activities sacrificed in order of seniority regardless of worth? What became of the testing work that was supporting the newer developments in content and methods of teaching and supervision? What became of research, guidance, curriculum-revision work, and of child health work in its many phases? Where is the school survey, now so much needed? What happened to reading, writing, and arithmetic, algebra, Latin, and the older features of the educational machine? Were they all preserved? Whence came the demand for retrenchment? What leadership came to the schools from the state office and from the state institutions of higher education? Did the public lead or did it follow in the wake of the school authorities? As a matter of public policy, what happened to the school facilities of minority peoples?

For those responsible for shaping and directing policies and plans for education, there is the challenge: Can an understanding of these depression experiences be brought to bear in the formation of a recovery program? The answer is: Certainly not until the effects of the depression have been mined and classified, and their real significance understood. This is the task of research.

Chapter VIII presents problems having to do with school finance and business management. The field of finance is the point of direct contact between the economic depression and organized educational activities. Whether support came from the public treasury, public or private endowments, tuition charges, or from churches or other organized groups, it did not escape the changes that swept over the value of its resources or income in 1929 and the following years.

While the depression struck on all sides its effects were different in different cases, depending upon the nature of the source of support. Many independent institutions operate upon a relatively fixed income from invested endowments; others operate largely upon continuous earnings through tuition; still others operate upon current gifts and tuition combined. Public schools of all grades are supported only in a minor way by tuitions, fees and income from endowments and gifts. Since one important criterion of the worth of a revenue system is its dependability in times of stress, there is urgent need for a study of how these many sources of support have withstood the depression. What has happened to the income of all the many types of educational activities in this country?

Support from taxation for public schools is not alone a matter of where the money is raised, but what resources of the people are tapped to raise it. Personal and real property is still a major resource. With the general property tax other forms have come into use, such as income, luxuries, severance, and sales; each in varied form. The depression affected all these types of taxes. Did it affect one type more than another?

When money was so hard to get by any source, it was natural that school expenditures should be reduced. Here was a new experience for school boards and executives. How did they do it? Bonds had been easy to vote in the past and they were readily marketable at a good price. Credit of school districts was giltedged. School bonds were the best of all municipals. What did the depression do to these securities? What happened to school-district credit? What happened to school debt payments?

Never has there been a more propitious time than now for a study of methods of taxation for school support; *general tax and appropriation* as compared with an *earmarked tax* for schools; whether a *statutory* or *constitutional* control of support is better; and methods by which the law fixes the amount to be raised for schools. The fields of debt and of budgeting a retrenchment program offer a chance to study the results of a severe test. There is exceptional opportunity to see what educational philanthropy and endowments can stand; what tuitions and fees will produce in such times.

In 1926 over 400 millions of dollars was expended for capital outlay. By 1935 this figure had dropped to slightly over 107 millions. In the meantime, enrollments grew from 24.7 to 26.9 millions.[1] This does not count the heavy inroads that were being made upon existing properties by the effects of wear and tear, and obsolescence. With education developing as it is, obsolescence is sure to become a heavier charge. It is a current question as to whether out-of-date housing is not actually impeding progress in curriculum development and in teaching method.

The depression brought a new kind of aid to school properties.[2] The federal government has entered the field of education in new and extensive ways. Each of these new enterprises should be reviewed for its own contribution and for its implications for local and state responsibility in education.

Chapter IX presents a few problems that have to do with what happened to the professional organizations and the scientific output of education. This is, for many reasons, an important part of this inquiry. There is every reason to believe that educators will build up and protect the educational interests of the country; that in times of distress this leadership will assert itself and warn of danger and advise where action is needed. If, because of their competency and readiness to serve, the country can rely upon medical men, lawyers, economists, engineers, sociologists, religious leaders, and educators to safeguard the well-being of these great divisions of public service, then democracy would seem to be reasonably safe.

---

[1] Facts are from: Report of the Joint Commission on the Emergency in Education. *Major Trends in Education.* 1201 Sixteenth Street, N.W., Washington, D.C.: National Education Association, 1934

[2] For a summary of PWA and other federal grants for education see: Covert, Timon. *Federal Grants for Education, 1933-34.* Leaflet No. 45. Washington, D.C.: United States Office of Education. 1935

What has happened to this educational leadership during this depression? Many phases of this inquiry fall naturally under the study of personnel. Here, however, the concern is with the profession rather than with the school staff; with scientific output rather than with the scientist. There are local, state, and national organizations of educational workers. These organizations center about various interests, scientific and professional. A stream of published material flows from them. At their meetings the problems of education are discussed. Scientific students of education attached to universities, research agencies, schools and school systems, are continuously at work on important educational problems. A continuous stream of official documents, national, state, and local, report the activities of schools and school systems.

The public very well may ask: What has the depression done to these workers, their organizations, and their work? A partial review of educational literature shows that little note was taken of the depression in 1929-30 and not much in 1930-31.[3] Who discovered the depression in education first? Was it school people themselves; or the lay public? What was the attitude of the profession toward the early signs of the depression? When did educators begin to study depression problems? When did educational organizations take note of it and begin to do something about it? This field offers an unusual opportunity to study what educational leadership can do to help the country by guiding its schools through a period of distress.

The problems have been presented here from the viewpoint of a theory and philosophy of education. The reason for including many of these will not be clear without taking these viewpoints into account. In searching for problems, it is necessary to

---

[3] There were noteworthy exceptions. As early as June 1930, J. W. Crabtree, for many years Secretary of the National Education Association, said in the Annual Report of the Secretary that the schools were facing a greater emergency than that following the World War. He called attention to growing fiscal problems, noted the oversupply of teachers, urged organization to hold the ground they had gained for education, and demanded government subsidies for education.

have some idea of what a problem is. To think only of what has been broken or destroyed causes too narrow a view. Even by tearing down what we have been long building, the depression may have been of great service at points. When challenged by serious loss or by a surprising revelation of weaknesses, new heights may be reached in the struggle to meet the issue. Even if issues have been answered stupidly or yielded to supinely there is need to reflect; for lack of ingenuity and courage would surely be a problem of the first order. Then, too, if the depression left education with broken support, broken morale, broken program, broken theory, and broken contacts with life, is the problem merely one of repair? Any student of social trends, as well as of social catastrophies, answers this in the negative. Hypotheses are not readily suggested by broken windows nor by broken ideals. They must be guessed from such signs as can be seen in the wreckage and in the struggle for reorientation taking place in the field of education. Thus there are many avenues of approach in searching for problems.

If by such explanations and interpretations as are here offered, the general student of social life or of education gains additional insight on education as a function of our society; if scientific workers find some illumination in their means of attacking such problems; or if any who browse through these pages find this amazing period thrown into better relief, this report will have served its purpose.

Index

Studies in the Social Aspects
of the Depression

AN ARNO PRESS/NEW YORK TIMES COLLECTION

Chapin, F. Stuart and Stuart A. Queen.
Research Memorandum on Social Work in the Depression. 1937.

Collins, Selwyn D. and Clark Tibbitts.
Research Memorandum on Social Aspects of Health in the Depression.
1937.

The Educational Policies Commission.
Research Memorandum on Education in the Depression. 1937.

Kincheloe, Samuel C.
Research Memorandum on Religion in the Depression. 1937.

Sanderson, Dwight.
Research Memorandum on Rural Life in the Depression. 1937.

Sellin, Thorsten.
Research Memorandum on Crime in the Depression. 1937.

Steiner, Jesse F.
Research Memorandum on Recreation in the Depression. 1937.

Stouffer, Samuel A. and Paul F. Lazarsfeld.
Research Memorandum on the Family in the Depression. 1937.

Thompson, Warren S.
Research Memorandum on Internal Migration in the Depression. 1937.

Vaile, Roland S.
**Research Memorandum on Social Aspects of Consumption in the
Depression.** 1937.

Waples, Douglas.
Research Memorandum on Social Aspects of Reading in the Depression.
1937.

White, R. Clyde and Mary K. White.
**Research Memorandum on Social Aspects of Relief Policies in the
Depression.** 1937.

Young, Donald.
Research Memorandum on Minority Peoples in the Depression. 1937.